The Stories of My Father

T. D. Roth

CONTENTS

ACKNOWLEDGMENTS

Special thanks go to my editor, Erin Linn McMullan. Erin's expertise and experience make for better writing and more enjoyable reading. Her ability to critique and encourage is a gift I greatly appreciate.

I will always be indebted to my stepmother, Lois *Rivers* Roth, for the loving home and support given to my father. Lois has a great eye for detail and graciously offered to proofread the final manuscript. It couldn't have been easy, because she sometimes had heard different versions of the same stories.

My greatest debt is to my father. He loved life and loved talking about it. Over the past couple years, we spent hours on the phone and in his home going through his life story. He passed away before this work was completed. If he could read it, I'm certain there would be changes. There is an African tradition that as long as we remember and talk about our ancestors, they live on and their spirits stay near. This is for you, Dad. Long may you be remembered for your sense of adventure and love of life.

AUTHOR'S NOTE

This is the story of my father, Gary Roth, *constructed from his favorite stories and my own personal memories.* It seems that memory is an enhanced form of fiction encasing a thread of truth. Perhaps that has to do with our efforts to make sense of events that we didn't understand when they first occurred. It might also explain why memories change over the course of time. I have no doubt that my dad embellished his stories, for they sometimes changed from one telling to the next. Consequently, *this is a story and not a history.* I've covered only the early years of my father's life, his marriage to my mother, Betty *Allen* Hartung, and the years that I lived with him as a teenager. I have supplied fictitious names for many people mentioned in this book. Because Dad lived in so many places and had so many jobs, the chronology and location of some events are questionable, but the basic story of his early life remains.

I loved the large cumulous clouds floating across the broad skies of southern Idaho. Sometimes I imagined ancient sailing ships crossing the vast expanse of blue to the exotic lands of the Orient; other times, various arrays of horses and soldiers marched across the sky to distant battles; occasionally, the faces of old men were transformed into laughing children slowly drifting away. Like life, the images were always changing, yet always moving, and never returning.

THE HAPPY WANDERER

YOUNG PEOPLE TODAY can't understand what it was like being born and raised during the 1930s. The New York Stock Market crashed in 1929. The deep plowing and over-grazing of the 1920s led to one of the greatest man-made disasters of the twentieth century, the Dirty Thirties. You've probably heard of farmers that were "dirt poor." We couldn't afford dirt, let alone a farm. My parents, Harry and Wanda Roth, wandered from one job to another and one relative to another trying to survive. In the late summer of 1931, Mom and Dad and my older sister, Jeanne, moved in with my Grandma and Grandpa Roth[1] in Twin Falls, Idaho. They lived in a small three-bedroom, two-story house. My uncles, Clarence and Jack, and my Aunt Opal also moved home that summer, so it was a houseful. My parents and sister slept on the screened front porch until the weather turned cold. That Christmas is one that I'm certain my mom never forgot.

The local church had given the Roths a food hamper for Christmas. With so many adults in the house, it's hard to believe they were that destitute, but times were tough. Even the church hadn't managed a turkey for the hamper. Grandma Roth put the food on the screened porch to keep cold until Christmas day. Somebody stole it. The family was so disappointed and looked forward to a dismal Christmas dinner of cracked beans flavored with a ham hock. Grandma shared their plight with a church friend who rallied the church to gather up another Christmas basket. This time they added a turkey. Christmas dinner was postponed until the day after Christmas, the same day I was born, December 26th, 1931. Mom later told me I was the most homely, scrawny little baby she ever saw. She felt she must love me a lot, because probably nobody else would and there were a few times when nobody else did.

Years later, I spent a summer with Grandma and Grandpa Roth. I had just finished seventh grade and had made my mark in football and baseball. I was strutting around as if I was really something. One Sunday after Church, Grandma led me down a lane to an old derelict house. The porch was sagging, screens ripped, and siding non-existent.

She said, "So, you really think you're something. That's where you were born! The weather was so bad that the wind blew through the cracks of the house. We had to shake snow off the bedroom blankets. If I hadn't been there for the delivery, you wouldn't have survived. It was over two and half hours before the doctor arrived to check you over and attend to your mother. Then your father refused to pay for the house call. He told the doctor, 'I'm not going to pay you. You didn't do anything. If anyone should get paid, it's my mother.' I've never been so embarrassed in my life. There's no shame in being poor, but don't you ever think you're something you're not!"

We lived with Grandma and Grandpa until I was about a year and a half old. Dad decided that prospects would be better in Wapato[2], Washington where my Grandma Baker lived. Off we went. Well, Mom's brothers, Clovis and Bill, and her sisters, Lola, Leta, and Letha, had all had the same idea. There wasn't room for four more people, so after a couple days we moved to an abandoned two-room house.

It was a frame house with one-by-twelve boards on the inside walls and no insulation. There were no cupboards or closets and no indoor plumbing. It might as well have been a barn. One of Grandma's neighbors loaned us an old stove that had been used outdoors to heat wash water. It was missing a leg and needed bricks to prop up one corner. I must hand it to my mom, wherever we moved she made the most of what she had. She stacked orange crates to the ceiling for kitchen shelves. She nailed crates together and gathered curtains around them to make beds for me and Jeanne. She even made little chairs. Over the few years she had been married, she had accumulated a small chest of pictures, curtains, and dishes that could be easily packed from one house to another.

I've been a happy wanderer all my life and if Mom took her eyes off me for even a moment, I was out of there. Even potty training posed a challenge. Who has time for that? If faced with a "big load," I just shook it out one pant leg and kept going. I was just coming on two years of age when she started tethering me to the clothesline. I learned quickly how to slip out of my little overalls and take off. Can't say those were the only times I made escapes without my pants, but I just had to see what was on the other side of the fence. That's part of my nature and always has been. Some hard lessons come with being a wanderer. One was how wooden spoons, small boards, and paddles feel on your backside. Believe me, those were lessons I reviewed many times over the next twelve years. I soon learned to weigh the joy of a new adventure versus the pain of the paddle. Stretching the truth followed quite naturally. Mom always said, "This is going to hurt me a lot more than it will hurt you." I figured it was better to tell a fib than hurt my mom.

Much of what I "remember" of those early years came from Jeanne. I do remember that we were always hungry. So quite naturally, we helped ourselves to some bright cherry-like fruit that was clinging to a neighbor's fence. An elderly Japanese lady, worried that we were eating poisonous berries, called the cops. When the black and white pulled up Jeanne was convinced we were being arrested for stealing. Both of us began wailing, which convinced the cop that we were reacting to the fruit. Off we went to the local hospital. The doctor confirmed that the fruit was nothing more than cherry tomatoes and perfectly harmless. Our next stop was the police station where we were held in custody until Dad came.

Toward the end of summer, 1933, Dad had a great stroke of luck. An elderly widower named Harvey Wilson owned a farm about a mile and a half out of Wapato. Mr. Wilson was no longer capable of heavy work and was looking for a family to live with him and run the farm. Dad had plenty of experience doing field work, working horses, and looking after cows. He had been raised on a similar farm in Nebraska before The Great Depression. We were given the run of the house. According to Mom it was one of the nicest homes we ever lived in as a family. There was a living room, a den, and a large kitchen. Jeanne and I delighted in helping with the chickens and running around the yard and garden. Mr. Wilson loved kids and was just like a grandpa to us. He read books with Jeanne and told her stories. He had a bit of an ornery side, too. I was very curious about Mr. Wilson's chewing tobacco. There's just something about "spitting" that fascinated me. Mr. Wilson decided to teach me to chew. I never did get into it, but he learned firsthand what projectile vomiting is all about.

The Yakima River was prone to flooding and in 1933 Wapato experienced the worst flood in its history. According to Mom, Dad and Jeanne had walked to town to attend a rehearsal for the church Christmas pageant. Mom watched the floodwaters coming closer and closer to the house. The road to town was flooded over. The water was edging higher and higher on the corn in the garden. No sign of Dad and Jeanne. What a relief when the back door slammed, and Dad came trudging into the kitchen. He was soaked to the bone. His feet were covered with mud. Little Jeanne was clinging to his back with both hands around his neck and her feet wrapped around his waist.

The first order of business was to save the cows. Dad led them out of the barn and tied them to the front porch. He dragged the pigs right onto the screened veranda. What a racket! Pigs squealing. Cows mooing. He set the horses free and left the chickens to fend for themselves. As the water continued to rise, Dad had to loosen the cows. When the water covered the porch, he turned out the pigs. The poor animals didn't have a chance. Later, their carcasses were seen floating down the river. One of the draft horses survived. The other became mired in the mud and had to be shot.

In the meantime, the basement filled with water and Mom's little trunk of treasures was destroyed. Two men rowing a boat from farm to farm showed up to rescue us. Dad loaded Mom, Jeanne, Mr. Wilson, and me into the boat and we were taken to an old school house where dozens of people were waiting out the flood. We only spent one night there. My mom decided we were going home. She would rather move the family to the second floor of Mr. Wilson's house than be surrounded by all those strangers with their crying kids, coughs, and sniffles. Dad and Mom had quite an argument over it, but she would not relent. A couple men got tired of listening to them and gladly rowed us home.

The house was dark: no lights, no heat, but also no water on the first floor. The wood on the back porch was a mixture of dry and wet, but sufficient to get the woodstove going in the kitchen. As luck would have it, our rooster had taken refuge on the woodpile. Dad bagged him, and we had roast chicken for Christmas dinner. The following day, December 26th, 1933, I turned two years old.

Wapato was in a state of devastation. The theater, the stores, the Post Office, in short, every building in town was filled with mud and debris below the second floor. Fences were destroyed; roads were ruined; bridges were gone. Though Mr. Wilson's house was still standing, what had taken him a lifetime to build was in a state of ruin. When the waters receded, he decided to move on and consequently, so did we.

Dad loaded everything we owned into a 1928 Chevy and we headed back to Grandma and Grandpa Roth's home in Twin Falls. My younger sister, Sally, was born while we lived there. I don't remember much about it, except that a little baby somehow appeared. Since Mom couldn't afford to go to the hospital, I assumed the stork must have dropped it off. People were pretty secretive about anything to do with sex and babies in those days. You never heard words like "penis" or "vagina." Little boys had a "weeny" and little girls had a "foo foo." Mom and I used the code name "Waldo" whenever discussing little boy hygiene.

In Twin Falls, Dad went into the cab business with a man named Phil Cargo. The Yellow Cab Company did well enough that they invested in several fruit stands and two International trucks. Dad then began making regular runs to Arizona and southern California to pick up produce. Soon our family moved into a large house in a good neighborhood. The house had plenty of space and all the conveniences, even indoor plumbing. Mom was able to buy new clothes for herself and us kids. She still enjoyed sewing but could buy her patterns and the quality cloth to go with them.

I loved playing in Dad's truck. I couldn't reach the

foot pedals, but I could twist the steering wheel back and forth and jiggle the gearshift. With a lot of "rrrrrrrrr" and "blmblmbm" I was making my own trips to California and Arizona. It wasn't long before I discovered a pearl-handled pistol underneath the seat. For any five-year-old, that was a find! I added police chases and cops and robbers to my drives. "Blam! Blam!" and "Kapow!" were quickly introduced to my acting repertoire, not to mention the occasional, "Owe, you got me!" It was only a matter of time when Mom caught me with the gun. She took the pistol and sent me to the house. When Dad came home that night there was a near brawl. She threw herself at him with both fists flailing and teeth bared. How dare he keep something like that where a little boy would find it! She called him a lot of other things that I don't feel free to write. Dad, being much bigger and much stronger, wrapped his arms around her and held her till she calmed down. I never saw the pistol again.

You've probably heard the saying, "You can take the boy out of the country, but you can't take the country out of the boy." Jeanne and I had been going barefoot all summer, but now that we were "well-to-do," we were expected to wear shoes to school. Shoes in the 1930s were not well fitting at the best of times. There was a breaking in period that usually included blisters on your heals, Band-Aids to protect the sore spots, and a period of general discomfort. Every morning we started out to school in our new clothes and new shoes, stopped at the corner of the house, hid the shoes behind a shrub, and then continued in our bare feet. On the way home, we stopped at the shrub, put on our shoes, and went into the house.

When the fall weather began to cool, the school principal dropped by our home one afternoon to speak to Mom. He must have been surprised that a family that lived in such a nice house couldn't afford shoes for its children.

Nevertheless, he expressed his concern. In special cases, the school would provide shoes for students in need. Mom was horribly embarrassed. She said she would look after the problem. The principal left, we were both given a good spanking, and the next day we wore our shoes!

Our neighbors must have wondered, "How does a cab and truck driver move his family into a middle-class neighborhood?" Late one Sunday evening, in the fall of 1937, the answer drove up to our back door. My uncle Ed took the occasional run to California for Dad. He had just come back from Sacramento and needed help processing a load of coconuts. He insisted it had to be done that night and that even the kids could help. Sally was asleep. Jeanne had homework. I was always game for a new adventure, not to mention that Uncle Ed offered me a nickel. I headed off to join my cousins, Jimmy and Bob, at the Perrine Hotel where Uncle Ed worked as night auditor. Uncle Ed backed the truck up to the hotel coal chute, dumped off the coconuts, and left. He then returned for his shift at the front desk. We were taken to the basement where tables with empty bottles and caps were waiting. Each coconut had been drilled, drained, and refilled with whiskey. Our job was draining the coconuts into the bottles. Can you imagine, I wasn't quite six years old and happily involved in a bootlegging operation. The Prohibition Act had been repealed four or five years earlier, but illegal booze was still big business. The fruit stands were perfect for laundering the money. Plus, people were willing to pay a little extra for shredded coconut with a hint of real whiskey flavor.

Over the years, Dad had done his share of farm labor, even taking us kids along from time to time. Whenever working as a foreman, he was very popular with the Mexican laborers. He made sure they got the occasional break and found that a shared bag of donuts did wonders for morale. Every morning Dad would drive the farm truck to town to pick up the men needed for the day. Men would almost fight to work for him.

Now that Dad was in the cab business, he remembered that Mexican migrants would pay generously for a trip from the fields of Idaho and Oregon to the orchards of California. Once there, they could blend with Mexican Americans and not be forced back across the Rio Grande after the harvest. So, Dad purchased an extended Dodge that had been used by a local funeral home to transport corpses. He converted it into a delivery van. He took me along on his first "delivery" to California. I was probably part of his cover. You know, a father and son taking a working vacation.

Just outside of Twin Falls, six Mexicans climbed into the back. They sang and laughed right up to the California border. Just before the border check, the singing stopped. The men were so quiet, they could have been a load of corpses. Dad covered them with a tarp and various boxes and supplies. He had made enough trips hauling produce to know the best times and places for easy crossings. Once past the officials, the Mexicans came back to life, singing louder than ever, "Ay, ay, ay, ay...Cielito lindo...." Never one to waste a trip, Dad continued to San Francisco to spend a week with a Chinese friend before loading our "delivery" van with fruit and vegetables to take home. I was only six or seven, but I was impressed by the friend's daughters. They seemed to be so nice and so beautiful.

That fall, the International came roaring down the back alley late one night. Dad rushed into the house shouting that we had to get packed and get out. Mom stuffed everything she could into the old truck and loaded three bleary-eyed children into the car. Dad drove ahead in the truck and we followed behind. As the sun rose on Twin Falls, we were crossing the state border into Ontario, Oregon.

Chapter Notes

[1]People had large families in the twenties and thirties and most families had a least one child that was "different." Grandma Roth had an interesting brother named Mont. According to Gary, his Uncle Mont was somewhat of an eccentric, always trying to come up with some new invention. He obviously wasn't concerned about making money, or he would have gotten a job. Mont became obsessed with the idea of creating a car powered by perpetual motion. To compound his mania, a vehicle he was working on started and crashed into his garage door. He spent the rest of his life trying to get it going again. That old Model T, with its extra flywheels, batteries, and generators deserved to go into the "Mad Scientist's Hall of Fame." Too bad he didn't understand the laws of thermodynamics; he could have saved himself a lot of trouble.

[2]Wapato is located on the Yakima River plain in a semi-arid, almost desert area of central Washington. Surrounded by rolling grassland with a spectacular view of Mount Adams in the distance, it is a beautiful place to live. With water taken from the Yakima River, it produces some of the finest potatoes and apples in the country. Outside the irrigated farmland is ranch country. Before World War II about half the population were Japanese. In fact, Wapato was second only to Seattle as a Japanese center in America when the Roths lived there. That changed during the war when the Japanese were forced to leave or sent to internment camps. The other half of the population was Caucasian, along with a sprinkling of Native Americans. The land had been purchased from the Yakima Indian Reserve.

A ROOM OF MY OWN

ONTARIO, OREGON IS located just across the southwestern Idaho border. Like most of eastern Oregon it is surrounded by the Great American Desert. The average summer high is in the 90s (Fahrenheit) with an annual rainfall of about ten inches. Because of the Snake River and the early development of irrigation, the area is known as the Western Treasure Valley, noted for potatoes, sugar beets, and onions. The town also holds one of the largest stockyards in the western United States, having brought in the Oregon Short Line Railroad in the late 1800s for shipping cattle to Chicago.

Nonetheless, in the 1930s prospects were just as bleak in Ontario as in the rest of the country. Dad was desperate for work and rarely home. Being poor, we learned how to make the most of every opportunity. I was only seven when someone dumped a load of onions in the vacant lot across from our apartment. Off I went with my little red wagon to sort any good onions from the pile. Then I headed down the street selling them from door to door. I must have been born a salesman, because I can sell almost anything and between sales jobs, my second-hand store, and garage sales, I probably have. Back in the day, everything my sisters and I earned went to Mom.

Uncle Clarence and Uncle Jack, Dad's brothers, came through Ontario that summer looking for work. I idolized my uncles. They were always up to something. The carnival was in town and featured a professional fighter that would take on all comers. The promoter offered $100 to any man that could take him. Dad and his brothers came up with just enough money for the entry fee. They had been wrestling and fighting from the time they were little boys and knew every move and trick in the book. Dad, being the stockier of the bunch, did the honors. So as not to look like a ringer, he was to take a good beating before putting the guy down. Dad and the boxer sparred and danced around a bit and then the fight was on. They punched, and they wrestled, and they rolled. The crowd roared. Dad started letting the "pro" get the upper hand. Seems everyone enjoys seeing a young fool take a good beating and Dad was getting pretty bruised up. He glanced at Uncle Clarence and gave him the Roth wink, the sign that he was about to go into action. After taking another good punch to the gut, he fell to one knee holding his stomach and groaning uncontrollably. The fighter, thinking the fight was as good as over, relaxed for just a moment and gave a triumphant grin to the crowd. Uncle Clarence gave Dad a nod and up he lunged, slamming an upper cut into the boxer's solar plexus. Boxer and crowd alike let loose one big "WHOOF!" It was fight over.

Clarence walked over to collect the money just in time to see the promoter jump into his car and peel out onto the highway. The brothers jumped into Uncle Clarence's 1936 Ford Coupe and the race was on. The cheat might have gotten away, but he had to slow down at the Cairo Junction about four miles southwest of Ontario. They forced him off the road, pulled him out of his car, and cleaned his clock. It made the beating Dad had taken look like child's play. When they finished, he was more than happy to give them their money, plus a little extra for their trouble.

Winter temperatures in Ontario usually drop into the low 20s and are accompanied with about a foot of snow. There are very few trees in that area of Oregon, certainly not enough for fuel, so most people used coal, which we couldn't afford. Mom gave me a couple small pails and I walked the railroad tracks picking up bits of coal that fell from passing rail cars. That wasn't enough to keep the stove going, so she sent Sally and me to gather cow chips from two large pastures that ran along the Snake River just outside of town. "Frozen or dried, but never fresh," was drilled into our heads. By mid-winter, we were using anything that would burn.

Sometimes there was no word from Dad for weeks on end. He generally found work on various farms and ranches but could hardly feed himself and earned only enough money to make the occasional trip home. Mom always put on an optimistic front to us kids. We were used to meager meals, but the day came when she called us to supper and set only three bowls of potato soup: one for Jeanne, one for Sally, and one for me. She had used the last potato and the last can of condensed milk. The next morning we went to school hungry. Then Mom dressed in her nicest dress, did up her hair, and applied a little make-up. She walked to the Rogerson Hotel and Restaurant and offered to work for free if she could keep her tips. I suspect we had other people's leftovers that night. My Mom was willing to do whatever needed to be done to feed us.

She didn't work there long. There was a small Chinese restaurant, the Hong Far, owned by Huey Hing. Huey offered Mom a small wage to go with her tips. This helped immensely but didn't cover all our needs. Huey was very frugal and expected the same of his staff. Leftovers went into a slop pail for a local hog farmer and were not to be taken home. Mom began having me drop by just after the lunch crowd, so she could slip a few scraps out the back door. We will never know exactly what Huey was saying when he caught her, probably only a Chinese sailor would, but it was loud enough to bring Louis Anchustegui out the back door of The Big Four Tavern next door. Huey took one glance at Louis and stomped back into the restaurant. Louis walked over to Mom and told her that no little boy was going hungry on his watch. I could come by his back door at lunchtime and there would always be a small sandwich and a glass of milk waiting. Jeanne and Sally were welcome too. Mom kept her job at the Hong Far, but she was shaken. She needed that job.

Louis genuinely appreciated Mom's struggle to look after us. He was amazed at the cotton dresses Mom made from large flour sacks for Jeanne and Sally. By the time Mom took out the seams, bleached the cotton fabric, and sewed her own patterns, you wouldn't know they were homemade. Louis gave Mom an old sharkskin suit for me. When Mom finished the alterations, I had the nicest pants in school. Some of the guys laughed at me, but I was proud of those pants. Louis became a very good friend of our family and I will never forget him.

Huey was different outside of business. He had paid $100, what seemed like a small fortune, for a Water Spaniel puppy for his little girl. Anytime the puppy came near her, she screamed and kicked the poor little pooch. Try as he might, Huey could not abate her fear of dogs, so he asked if we would like the puppy. What a great gift! We named him Andy. Andy was curly black with a small white patch on his chest. Once fully grown he would be a bit taller and deeper chested than a large Cocker Spaniel. The first order of business was to dock his tail, a common practice for spaniels and other hunting dogs.

These days, few people can imagine doing such a

thing at home, but Mom and I took little Andy to the chopping block behind our house. I was to hold him while Mom swung the axe. When the axe fell, I closed my eyes. Andy wiggled just at that moment and lost a piece of his little butt along with his tail. He lived his whole life with a scar about the size of an old-fashioned silver dollar. Only a little tuft of hair stuck out where there should have been a tail. Not having a tail to wag, Andy shook his whole rear end when he was happy, which he wasn't that day. He broke free, yelped for bloody murder, and ran under the house. It was three days before he was hungry enough to come out. With a lot of care and attention he became a great family pet. They say dog is man's best friend. I'd say doubly so for a little boy growing up during the Depression.

Since Dad was rarely around, it fell on Mom to raise us. She had lived for several years in the wilderness of north-central Idaho and felt it important that every boy know how to catch a fish, shoot a gun, and ride a horse. She helped me catch my first fish when I was about six years old. It was just a tiny little sunfish. Mom said, "Do you want to keep it? It's going to die if you keep it and it's too little to eat. If you throw it back, it will have the chance to grow big and have babies of its own." I threw it back and have always had a soft spot for animals. The rule is simple, don't kill anything you can't eat. Life of any kind is too precious to waste.

We didn't own a horse, so that would have to wait, but between Andy and my fishing pole, I figured I had it made. The Snake River was only minutes from our house and was my favorite place. The sparse cottonwoods and willows were a boy's paradise for exploring and building forts. In some areas the cheat grass and sagebrush came right to the edge of the rocky banks. All my friends went there with their fishing poles. We mostly caught carp and squawfish[1], which weren't considered edible, but if you knew where to fish, there were crappies in the sloughs and channel cat in the deeper holes. Occasionally I hooked into a nice trout. In our quest to get the "big one," my friend Jimmy and I decided to "borrow" a small cable ferry located northeast of Ontario. Our plan was to stop the ferry in the middle of the river, put our lines in the water, and wait for the big ones. What a surprise when the cable snapped, and the ferry floated downriver and grounded on a sandbar. We managed to hike home, but we never told a soul. Mom would have skinned me alive over that escapade.

Mom had a couple rules that I feared to break. Rule one was never go into the river. The Snake River looks wide and lazy running along the Oregon-Idaho border, but more than one little boy has been dragged down by its treacherous undercurrents. Rule two, I was not to be more than fifteen minutes from home when she was at work. On those days I was to leave Andy in the house. When Mom got home, she would turn Andy loose and he would track me down, usually within ten minutes. Once he found me, I had twenty minutes to get home.

Andy was very protective, and we always felt safe with him around. He would fight anything with four legs. He was still a young dog when I heard a vicious fight erupting in our back yard, followed by a "ki-yi-yi-yi." A huge German Shepherd bolted around the corner, running on three legs, followed by a Water Spaniel hell-bent on his heels. Andy had his own way of fighting. Unlike dogs that spar off, circle each other, and then engage, Andy always charged straight away. It gave him an instant advantage and he always went for a front paw. Even the biggest dog won't fight on three legs.

All my childhood I had shared a room with Jeanne and Sally. The girls slept at the head of the bed and I slept across the foot. As I was going into third grade, Mom decided I needed a room of my own. We moved into a house in an area called Speed Acres. My room was only about nine feet by nine feet and more of a closet than a bedroom, but it had a window high up on one wall, and most importantly, it was mine! I felt pretty grown up and wanted the same freedom other boys had. Mom had her own ideas about boys and freedom. One night I had been sent to bed while the gang was still playing in the park across the street. I could hear the radio playing in the living room and waited until Mom turned it off and closed her bedroom door. I quietly pulled a chair to the window and proceeded to slide out backward on my belly. Before my feet hit the ground, a large paddle connected with my bottom and I scrambled right back into the room. The last thing I heard was, "Now, stay there!"

Nineteen-forty was a terrible year for us. We had moved into a house on North West First Street, just across from the Christian Church in Ontario. Shortly after the move, Mom contracted diphtheria. The doctor could treat the symptoms, but there was no cure. If a patient didn't suffocate from scummy mucous filling the windpipe, there was still the diarrhea, vomiting, and often pneumonia to follow. There were no antibiotics. Mom's neck glands swelled to the point that her facial muscles were partially paralyzed. Then she temporarily lost use of both legs. She couldn't eat or keep fluids down. The health department posted a large sign beside our front door, "CARRIER OF **DIPHTHERIA** KEEP OUT OF THIS HOUSE." No one could come or go. Groceries were left on the front steps. Since no money was coming in, we ran up quite a tab on food and rent. It took Mom a couple years to pay off the bills after she recovered. Dad was working in Burns, Oregon, herding sheep for a rancher named Gus Davis. He only came home twice in the next several months to see how we were doing. He was barely making enough money to feed himself and was of little help. He certainly didn't come into the house.

The quarantine sign was down for a week when I fell sick. Back up went the sign. Between Mom's quarantine and mine, I missed almost a whole year of school. During that time Jeanne took it on herself to teach me to read. When the quarantine lifted, I had to repeat the third grade. My teacher commented on the first report card, "What happened? He can read!"

You would think that having almost lost me, Mom would have become over-protective, soft, and gentle. That was not the case. Even though married, she was virtually a single parent. The only way she knew to protect us was to keep us in line. I don't doubt that she would have done anything for us, but her love was generally expressed with a belt, paddle, or switch. I got a licking at least twice a week. I don't mean just a gentle pat on the wazoo. Mom took a belt or switch and worked from the back of my legs to the base of my neck. One time I had seven whippings in six days. I don't blame her. I could be the most provocative kid.

I once put a snake under a cushion just as Sally was about to lie down. I'd stare across the dinner table at Jeanne and say, "What's that spot on your face?" I knew she was sensitive about her complexion and we would soon be fighting. We went through a stage of telling on each other just to get the other person in trouble. Mom grew so tired of our squabbles that a new rule came into play. The culprit and the tattler would both share in the licking. I was so ornery I would sometimes tell on Jeanne, ask to get my spanking first, and then stand outside the door and laugh when she got hers.

Sally was different. She was the sweetest, most helpful little sister anyone could ever have. She rarely got spanked and I distinctly remember a spanking she missed. Sally and I had gone to a movie. Since there was rarely enough money for such a luxury, when we did see one, it was a great treat. Normally a show began with trailers of upcoming attractions followed by a cartoon. Bugs Bunny, Daffy Duck, and Betty Boop were some of our favorites.

After the cartoons there was a newsreel. At that time, we would have seen the latest (only several weeks old) stories of failing farms, Roosevelt's New Deal, and Hitler's rise to power. I'm almost positive the newsreels were designed to bore kids to death. Then came the main feature. Sound was still in its infancy and most movies were filmed in black and white. I don't remember what we saw, but movies like *Dracula* and *King Kong* were great hits with the boys. John Wayne starred in the early westerns. *The Wizard of Oz* came out in 1939. The theater generally ran two features, so once you were in, you could stay for both.

I came home after the first feature. It was already dark, and Mom wouldn't allow us to stay out late. She was in bed and called me into her room.

"Where's your sister?"

"You mean she's not home?" I wanted to cover for Sally.

"No, she's still at the show, isn't she? You go get her."

Sally was only seven or eight years old. I found her sitting in the back row with her legs crossed. She was such a good sister, always willing to help, and never causing any problems. She loved reading and she loved stories. It's no wonder she stayed. When we came home, Mom called us into her room. She didn't even bother to get out of bed. She just reached down for a slipper and pulled Sally across her stomach.

I grabbed the slipper as her arm came down and said, "You want to beat on somebody, beat on somebody who can take it!"

Mom came out of that bed and gave me the worst licking I ever had. When she finished, she held me by both shoulders and glared into my eyes, "You want to take any more for her?" I think Sally cried a lot harder than I did.

As I entered fifth grade, I had a bout with strep throat. The strep eased up, but my knees and elbows began to swell and ache. My stomach hurt. I ran a constant fever. I had no energy and could hardly eat. Old Doc Lawrie came to the house. I said, "ahh" as he stuck what I thought was a Popsicle stick into my mouth. He shined his little light up my nose and into my ears. I nearly went into shock when he placed that COLD stethoscope on my chest. "Breath in and hold your breath," he said. "Now blow it out." Dr. Lawrie seemed to spend forever listening to one spot after another. Finally, he wrapped up his stethoscope and placed it in his bag, "Wanda, come with me. We need to talk."

The doctor led Mom into the next room. I immediately crawled out of bed and did what any eleven-year-old would do. I put my ear to the door.

"Wanda, I don't know how to soften this. Gary has all the symptoms of rheumatic fever. It's already attacking his heart and there's nothing I can do. Based on his decline, he probably doesn't have that much longer to live." I heard Mom stifle a sob as he continued, "I'll be here to help you through it, but that's all I can do."

Mom broke down crying and so did I. She must have heard me because my bedroom door burst open, and she took me by the shoulders.

"You're not going to die! I won't let you die!"

"But the doctor said...."

"Doctors don't know everything. We'll bring your Grandma Baker. She'll know what to do."

I didn't have a lot of faith in Grandma Baker. She might know all about mustard plasters, forest herbs, and Indian remedies, but she wasn't a doctor. I passed word to my friends that I was going to die and began giving away my collection of boyhood treasures: things like my pocketknife, my fishing pole, and a stash of comic books. The guys were sad, but quite ready to help divest my "fortune."

Grandma arrived, and I soon thought I would die from the taste of her potions. Holy cow! The smell of her concoctions was enough to make a boy get better just to escape. My fever came down, my heart slowed down, and my energy gradually revived. I've suffered with angina and other minor heart problems over the years, but thanks to my Grandma Baker I've lived a lot of life since.

I never did get all my things back. The guys accused me of being an "Indian Giver."[2] Guess it doesn't pay to always believe what the doctor says.

Chapter Notes

[1]"Squawfish" has become a politically incorrect term. The fish, which are prolific in western North America, are becoming known as "pikeminnows."

[2]The term "Indian Giver" was a common slur against Native Americans. It signified a person who gives a gift and then takes it back. It is interesting that whenever American Indians have tried to regain land, property, and homes from the white population, it has been an effort to regain what was stolen or shared, never something freely given.

ON THE LAM

FARMING WAS DIFFERENT in those days. There was always summer work for boys on the farms and ranches around Ontario. Most crops required irrigation by means of canals, ditches, and siphon tubes, all requiring manual labor and regular application. Ranchers needed extra hands during haying and harvest. By age nine I was helping a rancher named Mel Greaves. We were moving a herd of cattle that bolted and ran me down. Mel felt somewhat to blame, so he helped me get my social security card and a job running tickets at the local stock auction on Wednesdays and Saturdays. Since Ontario was a shipping center for cattle and maintained large feedlots, the auctions were big business for the surrounding area. They paid me a dollar a day, good money for those times and unheard of for a little boy. Mel must have realized how much our family needed the money.

Meanwhile, Dad returned home and decided to resurrect his trucking business. Whatever had happened in Twin Falls had blown over and we still had one old International truck. It had been parked for a couple years, but still had a lot of life in it. Instead of running his own fruit stands, he began selling to small markets and grocers. No more rum running and no more "taxi" service to California. Mom wanted to work with him. She was excited about taking orders from local grocers while Dad made the runs to Arizona. So, Dad headed for Arizona and Mom began making the rounds to local markets. Mom was good at sales. By Dad's second trip, she had a full order of pre-sold fruit and vegetables for Ontario and the surrounding area. As Dad returned from Arizona, he ran into old friends in Twin Falls and sold the entire load. He drove back to Ontario with an empty truck. Mom went back to her customers promising their orders on the "next" shipment, only to be disappointed again. After the third trip she was too embarrassed to continue.

A woman called "Little Wanda" moved into Ontario about that time. She was from the previous era of speakeasies and brothels. Ontario seemed like the perfect location to set up a classy establishment for entertaining men, but Little Wanda needed help. Dad was rarely home, and Mom was desperate for money. She was not the type to peddle her body, but she was not above decorating and remodeling for Little Wanda. Mom had plenty of experience setting up one home after another over the years, was a good seamstress, and had an eye for color and texture. She taught me how to clean windows with vinegar and newspaper so I could help. As I understand it, Dad happened to come home while Mom was working for Little Wanda, accused Mom of working in a brothel, and filed for divorce.

The next thing I knew, Dad loaded us kids into the truck and headed to Twin Falls where we moved in with Grandma and Grandpa Roth. They had already raised a family of eight and were too old to take on three more, ages thirteen, ten, and eight. Since Dad was gone most of the time and couldn't look after us himself, Sally and I soon joined Mom in Salem, Oregon. Jeanne joined us a year or so later when Mom moved to Payette, Idaho.

We weren't in Salem long when Mom met Charlie Bates. Charlie showed her the attention and fun she hadn't seen in years. They married and dropped me and Sally at Grandma Baker's in eastern Washington while they set up house on a military base near Vancouver. This would have been about 1942, partway into World War II. Bates worked for the Kaiser Shipbuilding Company[1], which played an important part in the war. Of course, we loved the time with Grandma Baker. Grandma had done just about everything you can imagine. At one time she had her own homestead in Colorado. She rode, hunted, and fished like an Indian. She knew all the native plants and cures. I thought she was Indian. She had followed her boys to the coal mines of Oklahoma and ranched in the wilderness of Idaho. She was also a great storyteller of times going back to the Civil War and settlers coming across the plains.

Mom's brothers, Earl[2], Vernon, Clovis, and Bill[3], either lived with Grandma or nearby. They were rough and tumble loggers who played just as hard as they worked. Wednesday nights and Sunday afternoons were dedicated to cockfights. This entertainment went well with hard liquor and the occasional cockfight of the human variety.

One night Uncle Bill staggered home in the wee hours of the morning. He shed his clothes and somehow managed to pass out between the mattress and the old-style coil springs. Next morning, his chest and one side of his face were covered with the circular imprints of the springs. Blood was oozing from a half-dozen or more places where the wire had cut into his skin. He looked so miserable and comical that we laughed and laughed. Uncle Bill didn't think it was funny.

Grandma took me with her to collect cascara bark in the surrounding forest. Cascara, known as "chittem" by the Chinook Indians, had been used for centuries as a laxative and could be sold to the local drug stores. Grandma was no longer into climbing trees, so I would scramble up the tallest tree around, look for the next cascara tree, and lead her to it. She was impressed by my enthusiasm and hard work. With the money I earned, she bought me a Winchester Ranger pump action .22 rifle. It quickly became my most prized possession. The pump action was perfect for a left-hander like me.

One morning I ran into Grandma's kitchen with a terrible case of the familiar, "Hic! Hic! Hic! Hiccough!" I held my breath until I turned blue. "Hic!" I drank water until I was about to drown. "Hic!" Grandma turned from the sink and frowned at me.

"Honey, why did you say those terrible things about me?"

"What things, Grandma?"

"You know what you said!"

I would never say anything bad about my grandma and soon began crying. Then she started crying. When we dried our tears, the hiccoughs were gone.

At summer's end Sally and I joined Mom and Bates. I insisted that I wouldn't go without Andy. Mom relented, much to her regret. As we were driving into Vancouver, Washington, Andy jumped out the car window and attacked a Labrador retriever. The Lab's owner tried to pull Andy off and received a severe bite to his right hand. Someone called the police. Andy was taken to the pound and the dog owner went to the hospital. Because of Andy's behavior and the fear of rabies, the local judge decided to put him down. Andy wasn't just a dog; he was the closest thing I had to a brother. I had to rescue him, no matter what! That night I climbed up the chain-link fence surrounding the dog pound. Andy never wagged his furry little butt for joy like that night. We slipped out the front door and headed for the hills. I didn't have much of a plan, but I had to save Andy.

We hid for three days in the woods. Like most outlaws, having crossed one line, it was easy to cross the next. Without my .22 and my fishing pole, living off the land was impossible. I had no matches, no blankets, no nothing for wilderness survival. Andy could catch the odd rabbit for himself, but that still left me cold and hungry. Low-level theft was my only recourse. I started spying on loggers working in our part of the woods. They weren't too happy to find their lunches missing, but a boy and his dog must eat. I couldn't stay "on the lam" forever. I finally came out of hiding, but I did get another day before the judge. With a lot of stammering and a few tears, I made my plea. Fortunately, the judge had a soft spot for boys and dogs. Andy wasn't showing any symptoms of rabies and would be given a reprieve if we sent him to Grandma's.

Mom's marriage didn't last. Bates loved Mom but found that looking out for two kids was not what he had imagined. I don't know what happened, but we were left high and dry with no money and no place to go. A friend had written Mom that a job was waiting in Emmett, Idaho. Mom sweet-talked a railroad engineer into letting us ride in the caboose of a freight train headed to Boise and we were soon on our way.

The job in Emmett wasn't there when we arrived, but Mom had contacts in Payette, Idaho where she had taken orders for fruit and vegetables. She quickly picked up a job as receptionist at City Cleaners. Her biggest problem was the low wage. This became an even bigger problem when Jeanne joined us.

To save money, Mom walked home every noon for lunch. One beautiful summer morning, Norm, Buzz, and I were playing football at the local park. We rushed home for lunch and tramped into the house just as Mom was setting the table. I'm sure she wasn't impressed by the fact that I would bring friends home for lunch. It was hard enough feeding her own kids, let alone someone else's. Mom frowned and said, "I forgot to bring home the bread...."

I was in a hurry to get back to the game and wanted to show off to the guys. I certainly didn't want to waste time going to the store. I interrupted, "Well, don't you think that was silly? Walk right past...."

I never finished the sentence. In the corner of the porch were thirteen lathes, a baker's dozen, that we boys used as swords in neighborhood battles. Mom broke twelve of them on me, threw the last lathe into the yard, and said, "Now, go get the bread!" Norm and Buzz were wide-eyed and shaking in their boots. They jumped on their bikes and took off. I headed for the store. Mom demanded respect and she would get it one way or another.

Years later I asked her, "Why were you so severe with the lickings?" She confessed some regrets but explained how alone she felt and how fearful that something might happen to one of her babies. Strict discipline was the only way she knew of keeping control. She went on to say, "Two times in your life, you came to me and said, 'Mom, I think I need a licking.' I thought if you asked for one, you must really need it." Lord, did she ever give it!

Of all the uncles, my dad's brother, Clarence, was by far my favorite. He was probably the best looking of the brothers; he liked nice cars; and he dated beautiful women. It seemed that he had a new girl every time he came home, and they were all lookers. Uncle Clarence sailed with the Merchant Marine. His tales of the sea and different ports of call resonated with my dreams of adventure. Occasionally, I caught bits of conversations not meant for young ears: conversations about exotic women and strange places. Clarence conveniently omitted the hard work, tedium, and boredom experienced between ports. I was convinced the life of the sea was the life for me. I could hardly wait for the day I could join the Navy.

The attack on Pearl Harbor by the Japanese on December 7th, 1941 had occurred just before my tenth birthday. Inquiries about Uncle Clarence confirmed that his ship was in Honolulu during the assault, but Clarence was nowhere to be found. As the weeks passed, the family began to believe that Clarence was at the bottom of Pearl Harbor. Late the following spring, my cousins spotted a man dressed in a pea coat and knit cap walking toward Grandma's house.

"Grandma! Grandma! It's Uncle Clarence! He's coming to our house."

"That's no way to tease your old Grandma, unless you two want a good whipping."

Grandma was doing dishes and watching out the kitchen window as the man passed. *Oh God, wouldn't that be nice...Oh God...Oh God.* The man turned at the gate and started up to the house. Before he reached the steps, Grandma rushed out the front door, caught him in her arms, and began to cry. "My son, my son. God has brought you home."

The tramp freighter Uncle Clarence had signed on was in Pearl Harbor during the attack. It was carrying massive culverts used in the construction of large highways. When Japanese Zeroes strafed the docks and released the bombs, the captain of his freighter ordered the crew into the large culverts. The culverts were then rolled down ramps onto the dock to get the men off the ship. By the time the freighter reloaded and finished its tour, several months had passed. Communications weren't good at the best of times in the 1940s. Clarence had assumed the family would know he was alright.

Apart from Uncle Clarence's experience, World War II had little impact on our family. Dad was too old to enlist, and I was too young. I was aware of the older brothers of my friends going off to fight. The white service flags with blue stars representing husbands and sons in active service began to appear on the walls and in the windows of different homes. Gold stars, representing sons and fathers who were killed, soon followed. Still, as twelve and thirteen-year-old boys, the war "over there" seemed like a great adventure. We loved pretending to drive tanks and fly planes and storm the beaches of the enemy. Mom could listen out the back door and hear the "dakka-dakka-dakka-dakka" of our pretend machine guns and the "ssssss...badaboom" as we pretended that enemy bombs were falling. The *Captain America Comics* came out in 1941. Captain America was our superhero, fighting the wiles of Adolph Hitler and the Nazis. *Military Comics* introduced Blackhawk and the Blackhawk Squadron, a multi-national squad fighting against tyranny and oppression. Victory Gardens and rationing were hardly noticed in our home. Mom was already serving fresh meat only once a week. She had been canning without sugar for years. Even with a ration card, we couldn't afford gasoline.

One thing about small country towns like Payette, the sports teams are always short of players. I learned, better to be a big frog in a small pond than a small frog in a big pond. Payette had a population of only 3,600, but it had a top-notch ball field. Walter Johnson Memorial Field was well groomed and had a large covered grandstand. One of our future claims to fame was Harmon Killebrew, nicknamed "The Killer" and "Hammerin' Harmon." When he retired in 1975, he had the record for the most home runs hit by any right-handed batter. As I entered high school ball, Harmon was entering Little League. Payette regularly produced championship teams in our division. I was left-handed, a good first baseman, and a good hitter.

Football was a different story. I wasn't that bad, but I wasn't that big. In one of my first scrimmages, I came up against a tackle named Brent Mosley. When Brent came off the line, he came up with both forearms into the side of my helmet and accidentally stuck his thumb in my right eye.

The world looked quite different with my eyeball dangling on my cheek. Holy cow, that guy was mean! Too bad he didn't save it for the games. The doctor managed to reset the eye, thank God.

Payette hadn't won a football game in twenty-two years. About mid-season we won a game against Fruitland, Idaho, population 1,200. Beating the poor little Fruitland team was not a big deal to any other team in our league, but that didn't matter to us. Payette High School, home of the Payette Pirates, was jubilant. We loaded students into a few cars and the back of a couple pick-up trucks and paraded through town, honking the horns and yelling for joy. I don't remember winning another football game while I attended school there. Of course, I was expelled the following year. In the meantime, I was making life-long friends. Norm Potter, Buzz Boemer, and Dick Cochran would share my adventures and heartaches for the next five decades.

During my Payette years, Dad moved to an 80-acre farm near Ontario, Oregon. I began going back and forth on the occasional weekend. On one visit I was helping drive in fence posts. Dad was kneeling beside a post and put his hand on top to pull himself up just as I was coming down with the sledgehammer. Smashed three of his fingers. I could never outrun him, but I managed to get to the house before he caught me. Thank God Grandma Roth was living with him at the time. She stepped between us before he could get his hands on me. I'm probably alive today because of Grandma. She was hardly four and a half feet tall, but her boys would not cross her.

Dad had a girlfriend named Shirley who lived in Ontario. He walked to her house just about every evening. Occasionally I went along. One night we were walking and talking when Dad suddenly disappeared. I heard a thump, a groan, and "dammit!" echoing out of the ground. He had stepped into a dry well. It must have been ten or twelve feet deep and four or five feet across. Dad figured he could make his way up by bracing his shoulders against one side and his feet against the other. Every time he got to within a couple feet of the top, just far enough that I couldn't reach him, he'd slip and slide back down. Finally, I ran to Shirley's house to get help. I banged on the door, but before I could say anything, she asked if I would like some fresh cookies and milk. She always had something ready for Dad's visits. I forgot all about Dad. Shirley asked about school and girlfriends and the like. We had a great chat. As I was finishing my milk, she asked how Dad was doing.

"Oh yeah, Dad...."

Shirley got a neighbor and a ladder and back we went. She didn't make a peep about the cookies and milk. What a sweetheart!

Chapter Notes

[1]The Kaiser Shipbuilding Company was established by Henry Kaiser with shipyards located on all three United States coastlines during World War II. Kaiser was to shipbuilding what Henry Ford had been to automobiles. The Victory and Liberty cargo ships built by Kaiser proved a vital part of winning the war. While in operation, Kaiser shipyards produced 1,490 ships, 27% of the Maritime Construction contracts. Typical time to produce a Liberty ship was two weeks.

[2]Earl Baker was Sarah Baker's oldest child. He had helped his mother homestead in north-central Colorado around 1915. He built up the largest trucking company in northern Idaho in the 1950s.

[3]Bill Baker eventually gave up drinking and got into house construction. His company built many houses in and around The Dalles, Oregon

Gary on Right

Sally and Gary

Gary and a nice catch!

Gary and Andy

MIDGE

I WOULD HAVE DONE just about anything to have a horse. When I was seven, Mrs. Elwood, an older lady that lived down the street from Grandma Roth in Twin Falls, had a Shetland[1] pony named Shadow. Shadow was a little black stallion that bit, kicked, and snapped at anyone in range. Mrs. Elwood said that any boy or girl able to ride Shadow could have him. Eight or ten of us lined up for almost a week. Shadow was the meanest little horse you can imagine. Few ever managed to get on and none stayed on. I think the old woman must have hated kids. She watched and laughed and taunted. Finally, we gave up. Holy cow! That little horse was so mean that no one would have wanted him anyway.

Uncle Clarence tried the same trick on me with a stud horse he brought to Grandma's place. He told me I could ride it anytime I wanted, but no bridle and no saddle, just a halter and rope. I was determined to ride that horse. I would grab his mane, swing up, and get thrown off again and again. Dad and Uncle Clarence thought it was so funny. Sometimes Uncle Clarence would pick me up and put me back on that horse. He and Dad kept egging me on. I think they had a bet going on how long I would keep trying. I must have been bucked off at least twenty times. Grandma Roth, bless her heart, came out of the house and glared at them, "That's enough!"

After Dad moved to Ontario, he occasionally took me to the livestock auctions. He liked to look at the animals, talk with farmers and ranchers in the area, and pick up the occasional calf. Dad had a genuine soft spot when it came to horses. Maybe it came from the hours he had spent walking behind the old horse-drawn plows. One auction stands out in my mind. We had visited the corrals ahead of time to look at the horses. As the auction ended, Dad noticed they hadn't bothered to show a big black Percheron mare. She was an older half-starved horse, scarred from overwork and abuse, shy of being handled, and not likely to bring even a minimal bid. Dad stopped the auctioneer as he was leaving the arena.

"I want to see that black mare."

The auctioneer gave him a crooked smile and said, "No you don't. That old nag is done. She'll be lucky to bring a few dollars from the knacker[2]."

"I came here to see what was for sale and I want to see that horse."

The auctioneer winked at a farmer standing by and said, "Mister, if you can get her into harness, you can have her."

About thirty minutes later Dad drove her out in full harness. He had a way with horses. Lucky mare. Dad couldn't have bid on her. He didn't have a dime in his pocket. We named her Maude. With proper care and attention, Maude became a fine horse for Dad's farm. She understood verbal commands and knew her job. Coming to the end of a furrow with the plow, she automatically turned back to begin the next pass. After about a month on the farm it was obvious that Maude was carrying a foal. What a surprise when she gave birth to a little mule colt. Dad once locked the colt in a shed while using Maude in the field. The little guy managed to scramble through the window and ran to join his mother. He was so insistent that Dad finally let him tag along. Dad loved working with Maude. Whenever he took her out to plow, his rich baritone voice would soon be floating across the fields as he sang his favorite songs. I've never seen him happier or more content.

When I turned eleven, Dad took me on a drive to Fruitland, Idaho. On the way home, I sat on the trunk of his old '32 Chevy holding a rope with a little mustang named Midge trotting along behind. Dad had paid $50 for her and later bragged about having bought his kid a horse. The truth is, he had borrowed my summer's savings to make the purchase. I didn't get paid back, but I had my horse. Midge was a dark bay with three white stockings and a small star on her forehead. She weighed about 750 pounds and sported one crystal blue eye. The Indians call a horse with a blue eye a medicine horse, sure to bring good medicine to whoever owns it. Midge was good medicine for me and enriched my life in more ways than I can count, but she made me pay for every blessing. When that blue eye turned blood red, I was in for trouble. Dad insisted, "No saddle for the first three years." He figured if I learned to ride like an Indian, I would be able to ride anything.

Midge had her own ideas about being ridden. I had to snub her head to a tree to get on, a sure way to get glared at with the "red eye." As soon as her head was free, she stiffened her legs, sucked in a deep breath, and proceeded to buck like a rodeo bronc until I was on the ground. Once I was back on my feet, she would walk over and rest her head on my shoulder as if to say, "Come on, let's go." She then allowed me to mount and go for a great ride. I think she was making sure I knew who was boss. We replayed that ritual every day for about a year. It's a good thing horses have a weakness for sugar lumps and cut apples or I would have done a lot of walking. I soon found out that she could jump just about any fence around. One of her greatest joys was to be chased. I can't say that I shared that sentiment.

Dad's farm near Ontario and Mom's house in Payette were only about eight miles apart, so I often rode Midge between the two. One summer, Dad leased a bull to breed his cows. That bull was a mean old thing. One day, he broke loose and took off across the hay field. Dad quickly clipped a lead on Midge and swung on bareback. Midge was a great cutting horse and instinctively knew what to do. Dad drove the bull back into the pasture and then cut across a large irrigation ditch. As Midge lunged up the far side of the ditch, Dad slipped backwards into the muddy water. Midge lost her footing and slid on top of him, pinning him in the mud with just his arms and head out of the water. She just sat there, refusing to move. That horse could be so ornery! I could hear Dad calling, but I let him suffer for a couple minutes. I wanted him to learn that Midge was my horse. Once he started cussing, which was very rare for Dad, I started worrying about what I might learn when he came out of the mud.

I must say, Midge was a great teacher about horse etiquette. The most important lesson: you never walk up behind a horse. She would turn her head like a mule, aim, and flatten you with a well-aimed hoof. Meantime, Mom had married a cowboy named Lee Grimes. More about him later, but Lee knew all there was to know about horses. Lee tried every trick in the book to break Midge of that habit. He cross-tied three of her legs so she would fall if she kicked. Didn't work. He tied her back legs to the stall. Didn't work. He bagged her rear legs. Didn't work. He hobbled her. Didn't work. Finally, I learned to step into one of her front shoulders anytime I came up to her and never to get in range of a rear hoof. Running up and leaping on her from behind would have been a sure-fire way to eliminate any possibility of having kids. I have my own theory about the cowboy in the movies who runs up and leaps on his horse from behind or drops from the loft of a barn onto "Old Paint's" back. Midge would have crippled you if you were coming from behind. If you were jumping from above, she would have simply sidestepped and then kicked you silly. Movie horses must be either deaf or blind or both. If you aim a rifle between a horse's ears like they do in the movies, the release of pressure from the barrel will blow out both eardrums. So, when you see some cowboy that is exceptionally bowlegged, you know that he ran up behind a horse that still had its hearing.

I got pretty cocky and loved grandstanding. I could stand on Midge's back with both hands outstretched at a full run. One time I was showing off this trick while bringing in the milk cows. Well, Midge sidestepped, and I took a bad tumble. She took off and I rode home on one of the cows.

A certain freedom comes with having a horse. I remember riding in the hills surrounding Payette. Our dog, Andy, ran behind. Sometimes I would lay on a sand dune while Midge grazed on the surrounding cheat grass and Andy nosed through the sage. Fleets of cumulus clouds drifted over with the vague images of ships and dragons and strange faces. I often watched the clouds and dreamed of having a real family with both a mom and a dad. Like my dreams, the clouds took on different shapes and eventually disappeared.

An Italian girl named Carina Bianchi sometimes spiced up these rides. Carina loved riding and would join me anytime she could. I stopped at her house one time and knocked on the door, "Hello... Is Carina home?"

Her aunt called back, "Avanti!"

I stepped in to find Carina's aunt at the ironing board wearing nothing but panties. She had long dark hair, deep brown eyes, and big.... Well, I'll let you use your imagination. My face suffered temporary paralysis as my eyes popped wide and my mouth dropped open.

"What you looking at? You never see a woman before? This weather too hot for clothes. Carina is out back. Mind where you be looking!"

The clouds took on a different meaning that day.

Midge was more than just a horse, she was quite a friend[3]. Silly horse came right into the house looking for me one time. Nudged open the back screen, stepped into the kitchen, and walked through the living room. I think she would have come right up the stairs if she'd smelled me. It seems to me, that as long as a boy has a horse or a dog, he's never really alone. I was lucky. I had both!

Chapter Notes

[1]Shetland ponies were developed in the Shetland Islands northeast of Great Britain. Because they stand only twenty-eight to forty-two inches tall, many people think of them as miniature horses. They were bred to work: pulling carts, packing peat, and plowing farmland. With the coming of the Industrial Revolution, they made ideal pit ponies for the coal mines of Britain, and later, of the United States and Canada. Shetlands have been known to pull twice their weight under conditions where a regular draft horse would pull only fifty percent. They are generally good tempered, but without proper training can be stubborn, unmanageable, and testy.

[2]A knacker is a buyer of worn-out domestic animals or their carcasses to be used as animal food or fertilizer.

[3]When Gary married and moved to Milton-Freewater in west-central Oregon, his mother gave Midge to a young girl in Emmett, Idaho. Even though Midge was about 27 years old, she was still a fine little horse.

Gary and Midge

THE STORIES OF MY FATHER

BULL DURHAM

"MAMAS DON'T LET your babies grow up to be cowboys," goes the song. Willie Nelson might have added, "And don't let your girls grow up to marry one." When Mom served a beer to Lee Grimes in the Hotel Bancroft bar, she was smitten. Lee was as cowboy as a person can get. Even the Marlborough Man looked like a tenderfoot compared to Lee. He was rugged looking, smoked hand-rolled Bull Durham cigarettes, wrestled steers, and rode bucking horses. Seemed to me he could do anything I had ever dreamed. What boy hasn't wanted to be a cowboy? Mom had been on her own with three children for three years, longer if you count all the time Dad was gone over the years. She was totally prepared to join Lee on one of his stallions and ride off into the sunset.

They married just after the war. Lee was horse poor and rodeo crazy. He competed in bronc riding and steer wrestling throughout southern Idaho and eastern Oregon, but rarely brought home any winnings. For about seven years Mom's life was worse than before. Lee couldn't keep food on the table and sometimes moved our family to places where Mom couldn't get work.

One such place was Ross McKenny's ranch on Highway 52 southeast of Payette. The ranch had only 250 acres but was in rich bottom land along the Payette River. Field corn grown for silage sometimes stood higher than a man standing on a tractor seat. With good weather the fields could yield up to 225 bushels of feed corn per acre and close to 100 bushels of barley. Lee got me on as a ranch hand for the summer. I soon learned some hard lessons. Lee promised to give me $200 for working through the summer and free room and board for doing the chores. In addition to my normal work of irrigating hay fields, building fences, and working cattle, I also found myself mucking hogs, cleaning stalls, and milking cows.

Lee sold me my first saddle that summer. I paid $25 for a beautiful Mexican saddle with a deep seat, high cantle and horn, and free-swinging stirrups designed for bucking horses. I was doing a full pull on a fence post one day: that's where you lasso the post, wrap the lariat around the saddle horn, and ride away from the post to pull it out of the ground. Midge put muscle into the pull and the saddle buckled, jamming the horn into my gut and ribs. Lee hadn't told me that the saddle tree was cracked. I could have been crippled. I later found out he had only paid $12 for it because it needed major repairs. Everything Lee did seemed to work for his advantage, and I was too young to say anything.

We were still on the ranch when school started up that September. I remember walking the five miles to the ranch after a ball game to find Mom in the barn milking the two ranch cows. Lee had gone to the bar after supper, leaving the chores for me. Milk cows can't be neglected without seriously injuring their udders or causing them to dry up and Mom wouldn't allow the poor animals to suffer. So far as Lee was concerned, that wasn't his problem. Thank God for my mother.

McKenny had parked an old Model A beside the barn

for use as a dog kennel. It was mine for the asking. Even though the interior had been totally trashed by the dogs, I managed to get it running. Initially, I sat on a fruit box as I drove around the ranch. Later, I picked up seats and interior accessories from a "parts" car kept by Buzz. McKenny told me I was never to take fuel from the large tank that held gasoline for the ranch equipment, but I was welcome to the diesel. I found that if I started the old car with a whiff of gasoline in the carburetor, it would run on diesel, howbeit with a cloud of smoke and fumes. Mom gave me a few yards of blue-striped, heavy cotton cloth that I used to reupholster the seats, door panels, and ceiling. It was my first car and I was quite proud of it. I've been rebuilding and reupholstering old cars ever since.

At the end of the fall harvest, McKenny gave a check to Lee that included my wages. Get this, Lee held back $100 for "room and board." He conveniently forgot that I had done all the chores. The next summer I stayed in town where I paid $65 for room and board and had no chores. A job in the cannery was better than working on the ranch for Lee. Times were so different in the '40s. I was only thirteen and working like an adult, but still had so much to learn.

That year, Lee wintered Midge for me by simply turning her loose with a herd of cattle on the open range near Willow Creek in eastern Oregon. Come spring, she had six inches of hair covering her entire body and was full of thistles and thorns. She was as thin as the pale horse of the Apocalypse. Many of the cows had frozen or starved to death. If Midge hadn't been a mustang, she probably wouldn't have survived. Then, because she was hard to catch, Lee shackled a six-foot chain to her right front leg so she couldn't outrun other horses. Midge learned to throw that leg in such a way as to fling the chain ahead and run anyway. Lee might know horses, but he considered them to be tools: use them if they do their job; discard them if they don't.

Lee was into bronc riding and bull dogging and wanted to see how Midge would do as a hazing horse. The hazer is a cowboy that rides parallel to a running steer to keep it in line with the bulldogger and his horse. Midge loved hazing. She would lean right into a steer if it was getting off track. It wasn't long before I was making good money by renting Midge out for hazing. Cowboys would pay up to $25 to use her for a weekend. I was making more money than most rodeo riders. I always warned them, "Don't come up from behind and swat her on the butt!" Of course, cowboys being what they are, the odd one thought he knew better. When one limped back, wanting his money, I said, "I told you so. Guess you won't do that again."

Even though Lee was an expert horseman, I never let him ride Midge. He quickly took the lash or whatever was at hand to beat any horse that failed to perform. In a fit of anger, he beat to death the most expensive horse he ever owned, a beautiful Appaloosa stud horse named Comanche. Comanche, with his mottled coat and speckled eyes, was a true medicine horse if ever there was. He kicked Lee while being shoed and was dispatched with a shoeing hammer. Bad medicine for a beautiful horse.

When Lee's brother, Leonard[1], came home from the fighting in Europe, Jeanne caught the romance bug. They met and ten days later eloped. Jeanne claims Leonard was so easy to talk to, she just couldn't resist. Fortunately for her, Leonard was nothing like Lee. He wasn't a big man, but he was the right man for a young woman that was attractive, talented, and headstrong. He had been tempered by the war, knew how to stand his ground, and wouldn't put up with nonsense. Beneath that was a layer of compassion and understanding found in few men.

Because of the rural nature of the state, Idaho allowed young people to drive at age fourteen. I turned fourteen one day and had my license the next. I remember asking Leonard if I could borrow his car to take a girl to a movie. It was my first real date. It was winter, and Leonard said, "You can take it, but be sure to drain the radiator when you get home. I don't want the block to freeze."

On my way home after the movie, Mom and Lee drove up behind me. Lee told Mom, "He's using Leonard's car and Leonard doesn't know. You better take care of this." I tried to explain but was accused of lying. Mom was as upset at the perceived lie as she was about the car. She took a belt to me and beat me from my neck down and back up again. The next morning, which was a Sunday, Leonard and Jeanne came by the house for coffee.

When I walked into the kitchen Leonard said, "Gary, did you remember to drain that car?"

"Yes, I did. Just like you told me."

"I hope you had a good time. If you need it again, just let me know."

Mom looked at Lee and turned to Leonard, "Did you tell Gary he could take your car?"

Leonard took a sip of coffee, "Of course I did. He wouldn't take it without asking."

Mom started crying and asked me, "How many lickings have I given you that you didn't have coming?"

I let the question hang. I had taken quite a few. Mom was a person who acted first and asked questions later. I had willingly taken several for Sally. She was the best sister that ever walked, and I would have done just about anything for her. I had taken the odd whipping for Jeanne, though she generally deserved whatever lickings she got. She was hardheaded like Dad, and Mom had to keep an eye on her. Leonard changed all that. Hard to believe, I was fourteen years old, working before and after school, and paying room and board when I received my last licking.

Lee and I finally became good friends after I married

a little gal named Betty Allen. Sounds strange, but Betty and I sometimes double-dated with my mom and step-dad. They had a son, Bill, who was only two years older than our son, Terry. The boys grew up together. Lee introduced all our kids to the world of horses. Terry and Bill rode in the local parades. Vicki, our little girl, was on a saddle from the time she could sit up. By the time she was seven, she could ride just about any horse Lee had. In an auction ring Lee easily increased the bid on various horses by having Vicki show them. He gave all the cousins cowboy nicknames like Swede, Dutch, and Jughead. We shared family barbecues and holiday meals. When Lee and Mom "split the sheets," it was a loss to everyone.

Chapter Notes

[1]Patrick Grimes wrote about his father Leonard's war experience, *"We were members of the Church of the Brethren, an off-shoot of the Mennonites. [The Brethren believed] killing anyone was a sin. Dad joined the army in 1939 [as a cook] ...because there was no work due to the Depression. Grandpa was requested to disown Dad by the elders of the church in front of the congregation. Instead, Grandpa preached on the Prodigal Son. I wish I could have heard that sermon! No one ever challenged Grandpa about Dad being in the service again.*

When the War [started], many young men in the Church went to Conscientious Objector camps, returning a short time later saying that most of the men [in the camps] were not there for religious reasons. [Some] men joined the services as medics or [took] other non-combat related duties.

Dad received the Silver Star with V (valor), two Bronze Stars, and a Purple Heart. While in a military hospital he was scheduled to be shipped home due to his wounds. Instead, he went AWOL [and returned] to his unit at the front."

Several years after returning from Europe, Leonard was confronted by a church elder for playing cards (another church taboo at the time) with his family. So far as this writer knows, that ended any family involvement with the Brethren or any other church. After witnessing the horrors of World War II, a hand of pinochle seemed petty and irrelevant to anything of spiritual importance.

COMING OF AGE

SEX WAS RARELY talked about in the 1930s and '40s. As teenagers, we never used the "F" word. We were shocked when we found out what it meant! Why would anyone want to do that? Somehow, your thinking changes when you hit twelve or thirteen years old. You become much more interested in watching the cows and bulls in the barnyard. Andy's antics with the neighbor's dog took on a fascination all its own. Of course, watching the family dog leaves the actual mechanics of lovemaking somewhat confusing. The girls, formerly excluded from our "boys" club, became objects of great interest. Mail order catalogues like Sears and Roebuck were sought out for the lingerie and brassiere sections. A few well-worn *National Geographic* magazines were hidden and shared, but Borneo bush women were not a great turn on. Like most twelve- and thirteen-year-old boys, we had tons of questions, but couldn't imagine asking our dads or moms. Surely, they didn't do that sort of thing.

After a couple years of intense curiosity, the sharing of distorted ideas, and a longing for "hands-on" experience, I was spending a night in Ontario with a buddy named Jerry Palmer. Jerry's home sat on a large lot adjacent to an older two-story house. We noticed cars coming and going and heard laughing and music coming from the upstairs rooms next door. The roof of Jerry's house looked right into the windows of the second-floor next door, so it seemed only natural to climb up the willow tree in the backyard, swing onto the roof, and have a look. Through one window stood a fully grown, well-developed, naked woman. Then a naked man, in all his glory, appeared and...well, it was something you had to see to believe. Jerry lived next door to a brothel.

We limited our discovery to a handful of trusted friends and nearly wore out the tree as we ascended the rooftop night after night. One pair of binoculars was passed from guy to guy for a closer view of the action. With summer temperatures regularly hitting over ninety degrees in eastern Oregon, all the windows and shades were wide open, and so were our eyes. Sometimes "guy" humor got a bit out of hand. Quite common were comments like, "Is that your mom?" with the retort, "Do you want a knuckle sandwich?" It would have been far more likely to see one of our dads. We didn't know any of the women, but we did recognize a few of the men. It wasn't long before we thought we knew all there was to know about sex. The problem was how to get some "hands-on" experience. The solution was my savings, sixty-two dollars and seventy-five cents.

One Friday night, we watched the house until all the patrons and cars left and then made our move. We had made it into the living room before the madam, Kitty Storm, realized we were only fifteen or sixteen years old. A couple skimpily clad women sat on a sofa. Two more stood by a small bar. Kitty took on a matronly role by giving us a lecture and telling us to leave. I pleaded, "but we have money," and waved a ten-dollar bill.

One of the women said, "Come on Kitty, they're kind of cute and things are slow. Let's have some fun. I think we can teach them a thing or two." That was an understatement! Jerry was sitting across from Kitty and nearly went cross-eyed when Kitty slowly drew one foot up on the sofa. Her dress slid down her thigh revealing a dark triangle of feminine pleasure. Jerry's fate was sealed.

A girl would give you a ride for two dollars or a trip around the world for seven. By Sunday morning we had visited both brothels in Ontario and another two in Weiser, Idaho. My money was spent. Mind you, I lent much of it to the guys, so I can't brag. We knew a lot more about the "world" at the end of the weekend than we did the previous Friday.

As the war neared its end, the Grand Coulee Dam project in central Washington was adding an expansion called the North Dam. They were paying eighty cents per hour (over six dollars a day), a fantastic wage at the time. I could make more in one summer than I had made in my whole life. You had to be eighteen to work there. I was only fifteen, but I had a plan. Young men were required to register for the draft at age eighteen. I managed to register and received a draft card stating that I was eighteen. Off to Grand Coulee, Washington I drove. I worked only three weeks before being laid off. The dam site wanted experienced, skilled labor. I had neither the experience nor the skill.

When I got back to Payette, I ran into Bob Estes one night at the Ritz Theater. Bob was an older student at Payette High School. He and Clyde Knowles were planning a trip to Boise to enlist in the Navy. What a great idea! Now that I was "eighteen," the call of the sea beckoned. Foreign ports and exotic women were waiting. The recruiters in Boise took my draft card at face value. We were given bus tickets to San Diego and were on our way.

Boot camp was much different than I expected. It started with a thorough physical. Doctors examined our teeth, lungs, and heart. I can't remember ever seeing so many needles. Small pox, tetanus, and typhoid vaccines were standard. Shots for cholera, diphtheria, and typhus were waiting for sailors shipping to the South Pacific. Next, we were taken into a large room where everyone shed their pants, shirts, underwear...everything. There's a certain bonding that takes place in a cold room full of naked men. Yeomen passed out skivvies and uniforms. Everyone then lined up for buzz cuts from the navy barbers. There was no room for individuality. A few fellows were near tears as they lost their wavy dark hair that had once so "wowed" the girls. We all looked identical. I was given a hammock with a thin mattress and two mattress covers fondly known as "fart sacks." I also received a pillow, two pillowcases, and two blankets. A Sea Bag, stenciled with my name, held all my possessions.

As new recruits, we were The Boots. My official rank was Seaman Recruit, but I wouldn't have it for long. Boot camp for three farm boys from southern Idaho was a breeze. The 5:30 a.m. reveille would have been considered "sleeping in" on Ross McKenny's ranch. The morning drill, marching, and conditioning was intense, but having played football, performed with our high school marching band, and swum in the Payette River, I excelled in the training exercises. I had been shooting my own .22 rifle from the time I was nine or ten. The gun range was a piece of cake. What I hadn't expected was all the classroom time. The Navy has its own language for its officers and equipment. A rope was no longer a rope, but a line. You don't run to the right side of a ship, but to the starboard. The location of the quarterdeck, bridge, and hold are basic knowledge for any seaman. By the second week we were introduced to an obstacle course for simulated emergencies, fire drills, and first aid practice. It was almost four weeks before we were in a boat on real water. Basic training was somewhat like attending high school or Junior College. We had a football team, boxing matches, and band. Aptitude tests were planned for the final week to determine our assignments. I hadn't thought about it when enlisting, but a large ship or aircraft carrier is a city unto itself and offers every career imaginable.

With just a week of basic training to go, our Chief Petty Officer called me out of a line-up on the drill field, "Seaman Recruit Roth, step forward."

"Aye, aye, Sir!" Wow! I thought maybe I was getting a promotion already. I smartly stepped forward.

"Seaman Recruit Roth, is your mother's name Wanda Grimes?"

"Sir?"

"We have a letter from a Wanda Grimes about your age and recruitment." Then addressing two other recruits, "Escort Seaman Recruit Roth to his barracks."

The next day I was on my way back to Idaho. Bob and Clyde made careers of the Navy and eventually retired. With some of the trouble I got into afterward, Mom, in utter frustration, once muttered, "I should have left you in the Navy."[1]

I used the draft card to join the National Guard. Coming home in full uniform after my first Sunday of drill, I "marched" in to Mom and announced, "I've joined the army." Mom came out of her chair and glared at me, "You're not going anywhere!" Moms can be such a drag! The National Guard would have to wait.

Since I couldn't enlist, I set my mind to making money. Fletcher's Bunny Farm was going out of business. Old man Fletcher was willing to give me the rabbits, hutches, and use of his farm if I promised to maintain the place. The only hitch was the location. The farm was located on a three-acre island in the middle of the Snake River. I figured that was no problem. I could use Mr. Fletcher's rowboat. Midge was always available in a pinch. I must say, the rabbits were prolific. I was butchering forty to fifty every week. I also hand set an acre of strawberries. The future looked promising. Then came the flood of 1948. The waters were too rapid for the boat, so I made trips with Midge, rescuing bag after bag of rabbits. Apart from what was on the island, I had no hutches or pens, so I butchered the lot. Before the field and buildings submerged, I secured the pens to the few trees that grew on the island. All my labor was not lost. The floodwaters flushed and cleaned all the rabbit hutches. I pulled out any remaining debris and weeds from the cages and sold them for a profit.

That fall, Dick Cochrane, Jim Eckert, and I begged a week off from school to go elk hunting. I don't remember seeing any elk. I do remember drinking a lot of beer and playing cards night after night. The cabin was well stocked and occasionally one of us would slip out for more supplies, so we stayed not one, not two or three, but four weeks. Our main staple was pork and beans, which translates into clouds of invisible, yet unmistakable miasmic gas. You can imagine how we smelled by the end of four weeks with no baths, no deodorant, and seemingly unlimited flatulence. I could hardly stand myself, let alone Dick and Jim. It was so bad that one night while playing cards, each of us kept to our own corner of the cabin. Each guy would crawl to the center to play a card and then return to his corner before the next person played. The body odor was beyond description.

The weather got colder and colder. Food stocks got lower and lower. There was no choice but to go home. If we had realized all the trouble we were in, we might have stayed. Search parties had been looking for us, but we were nowhere near the search area. Police bulletins had been issued. Accidents and hospitals had been checked. When we returned, our moms broke into tears of joy and relief. The joy soon changed to anger and disdain. We were expelled from school for truancy. Dick started taking the bus every day to the high school in Weiser. Jim joined the Navy. I would have gone with him if I hadn't just been kicked out. Still, fate worked in my favor...or not.

I moved to Vale, Oregon to live with Dad and continue my junior year in high school. By this time Dad had married Dorothy Allen, a young woman about twenty years his junior. They had two little children, Sandy and Jud. Grandma Roth was living with them as well. Dot (Dorothy) and I became very good friends. She brought some badly needed stability into Dad's life.

Vale High School offered opportunities for football, basketball, and baseball. I had to work at getting good grades, but in another year and a half I might actually graduate. Miss Childs, my English teacher, was only twenty-two. It was her first year of teaching and I suddenly developed a great need for tutoring in English. I didn't fool Dad. He had gone back to school to finish high school at the age of twenty-one. His English teacher had offered to put him through college if he would marry her. He had declined, but he understood all about "tutoring." He wanted to make sure I finished high school and didn't do something stupid.

A farmer from Dad's church broke his leg about that time. Dad informed me, "You're going to help Jake Edwards until his leg heals." Jake had seven cows that needed to be milked morning and evening. I looked after the cows and set water on thirty acres of beets for the next two and a half months. Morning chores started at 4:00 a.m. I barely finished the chores before running to catch the bus and then showered in the boy's locker room at school. After school, I was at Jake's for the evening milking. There was no more time for "tutoring."

Tony and Chad Bosco, known as the "Bosco Boys," helped me set up a shoeshine stand in their barbershop. I sometimes made fourteen or fifteen dollars a week with that stand, more than some men were making at their full-time jobs. A lot of cowboys live in eastern Oregon and no one paid less than a dollar a shine for cowboy boots. Those that tried were shamed by the Boscos as "cheapies." With tips, I sometimes made $1.50, $2.00, and once, $3.00 for a boot shine. Cowboys love their boots and pay well for a detailed shine on a pair of dress boots. I paid Dad minimal room and board, and for the first time had money to spare. Cars were at the top of my shopping list.

I always kept two or three Model Ts: one to drive and at least one for parts. They weren't like owning a new car, but they were affordable and easy to repair. An older crippled fellow by the name of Ted Ferguson wanted my 1921 Model T. He was desperate for a car and short on cash. Dad convinced me to give Mr. Ferguson the car with a promise to pay me later. You can guess how that turned out. I didn't see him or the car for a couple months. One afternoon, a beautiful refurbished 1921 Model T was parked in front of Bosco's Barber Shop. It had been painted and reupholstered and looked fantastic. A few flaws in the body and marks on the dash reminded me of... Holy Moses! It was my car. I looked around, climbed into the front seat and drove home. If old Ferguson could afford a paint job, he could afford to pay me.

Within the hour, Ferguson and Sheriff Evans were at the house. Mr. Ferguson pointed at the Model T, "That's my car," then shook his finger at me, "I want him arrested!"

The fact that he would "steal" my car and accuse me of being a thief really got my goat. I told the Sheriff, "This is my car. He took it two months ago and never paid me. I'm taking it back."

Sheriff Evans scratched his chin, looked at Mr. Ferguson, looked at me, and said, "Do either of you have the registration to this car?"

I immediately replied, "I do, and I'll get it." I didn't have it, but I hadn't given Mr. Ferguson any paperwork when he took the car. I had the registration to a 1917 Model

T that I used for parts. The styles were identical, and the sheriff would have to take a very close look for the registration number. It was located on the block and not easy to see. Before he could check, Mr. Ferguson pulled a wad of bills out of his wallet and shoved them at me.

"Okay, okay, here's your money," he said. "Now give me my car."

I replied, "I've changed my mind. It has a nice paint job and new upholstery, and I want to keep it."

Dad interrupted, "Look, he's crippled and needs the car. You give it back."

"No, it's mine and I'm keeping it. He should have kept his part of the bargain."

The Sheriff handed me the papers, "I think we're done here. Take your registration, son, and enjoy your car."

I had started boxing as a freshman in high school and with Dad's help progressed into the regional Golden Gloves. Dad had his own ideas about conditioning. Contrary to my coach's instructions, he insisted that I have a large plate of mashed potatoes and gravy several hours before every fight. He claimed the potatoes fed the muscles and the gravy lubricated the lungs. It must have worked, because I was a good fighter.

As part of my training, Dad and I wrestled or boxed almost every night. The night before my last fight, we got to wrestling in the living room. Dad took me down, grabbed my right arm and planted one foot against my jaw and the other in my armpit. Then he started lifting me up and slamming me on the floor. One slam smashed my ear and I saw red. I broke his grip and took him down with a chokehold. His eyes bugged out, his face turned blue, and he was about to pass out when Dorothy jumped on top of me. If she hadn't, I might have killed him. I didn't notice it at the time, but Dad had stretched the muscles and tendons in my right shoulder. As a boxer, I was so used to aches and pains that I didn't pay much attention to the ache in my shoulder. I should have.

The following night I had a bout with a boxer some six inches taller than myself. Because he was tall and wiry and I was short and stocky, we were both considered middleweights. I was left-handed, but I always started a fight from a right-handed position, planning to switch over when an opponent least expected it. Dad and I had perfected the bolo punch with my right hand. The punch had originated in the Philippines and followed the same motion used for cutting sugar cane with a machete. It wasn't a knockout punch, but it opened an opponent to take a serious uppercut from my strong left arm. As I threw the bolo, the fellow threw a left body punch that glanced under my arm. He then flung his arm outward, forcing my right arm up and out. My shoulder, already weakened the night before, dislocated. It was a technical knockout. The guy won the fight without ever connecting a punch. To make matters worse, Dad and the coach took me back to the dressing room thinking they could put it back. All their pulling and manipulating proceeded to further stretch the ligaments and damage the bone around the socket. The shoulder was never the same afterward. Several years and eight dislocations later, I required surgery. I was fortunate not to lose the use of the arm, but more on that later.

Basketball season had ended, and baseball was yet to commence. Spring fever, with an indescribable yearning for action and adventure, hit as hard as ever. I walked into school on a Monday morning and opened my locker just as Bob Clauson and three other guys were heading out the front door.

"Hey Bob, where are you guys going?"

"We're planning an unscheduled trip to San Francisco to visit my cousin. Want to go?"

I threw my books into the locker and stepped in line. Why not take a couple weeks off before baseball season?

Two fellows who had been suspended joined us at the front steps and the seven of us hoofed it to the highway. The conversation was mainly about California girls. None of us had met one, but we had "heard" they were wild and willing. Forget about seeing the Golden Gate Bridge or looking across the bay at Alcatraz, just bring on the girls.

It was a hot day and we had walked less than a mile when Tim Bronson and Billy Scott decided that California girls were not worth being suspended from school. Besides, they didn't think we were serious. If they hurried, they could make the second or third period at school and get off with just being tardy. That left five of us. By this time, we realized that we were going in the wrong direction. We snuck back through Vale and headed toward Juntura on Highway 20.

Hitchhiking was common during the war years and people were quite accommodating. We managed to make the 55 miles to Juntura on one ride, but there was little traffic going further, and picking up one stranger is entirely different from picking up five. Plus, people are somewhat suspicious of five teenagers hitchhiking on a school day. So, Bob Clauson, Laverne Madison, and I hid in the brush. A truck stopped for Rudy and Johnny. They were supposed to motion to us to join them, but instead jumped in the back and waved as the truck pulled away. We wouldn't see them again for several weeks. Now we were down to three.

A big farm truck hauling seed was about to leave the service station at Juntura, but the driver wouldn't give us a ride. As he pulled out, we jumped into the back of the truck and ducked behind the seed sacks. After about a mile and a half the truck pulled onto a lane leading to a small farm. We would never get out of eastern Oregon at the rate we were going. We had passed a train yard coming out of Juntura and came up with a brilliant idea. Why not hop a freight? The right train would get us to California in just a couple days, so we walked back to Juntura.

A flatcar loaded with enormous glass panels seemed perfect. The panels leaned together forming a large "A", which was wrapped with heavy paper. We cut through one end of the paper and crawled into an empty, well-hidden space in the center. What could be better? We were protected from wind and rain; we were hidden from the railroad police; and we would soon be on our way. California here we come!

When the train pulled out and up the first hill, we felt a slow rhythmic "bump." As the freight gained momentum, the "bump" turned into a jolting "k'thump...k'thump...k'thump...k'thump." One wheel of the railcar had a flat worn spot. The ride soon became so rough that one of the glass panels cracked and splinters of glass began showering down. We were forced to our knees and held each other's hands to keep from bouncing wildly on the car deck. Soon, there were holes in the knees of our pants and toes of our shoes. Then the glass panels began to shift. We braced our backs against the sheets of glass to hold them in place. Bob began to cry and soon we all joined him. Laverne wet himself. There was no way to take a leak or shit without being thrown off the train. We were a sorry looking lot by the time our car was unhooked at a siding in Portola, California some 450 miles and twelve hours later.

What a relief! We had been dropped off on a siding in the Sierra Nevada Mountains. Crawling out of our "shelter" we saw fresh white snow covering the ground and surrounding mountains. We had survived! But we hadn't arrived, and our relief was short-lived. At that time, Portola was a crew change site for the Western Pacific Railroad and nothing more. No stores. No restaurants. Nothing but a locked shed and a switch in the tracks. Not that it mattered; none of us had any money. If it hadn't been for the snow, we probably would have died from thirst. We faced a day of snow and cold before another train arrived. This time we picked a flat car carrying three large pipe-like flumes. The three of us crawled into one of the flumes. We were in no way prepared for what lay ahead. A mixture of soot and ash from the coal-fired engine, mingled with wind and snow, whistled through the flume. We took turns laying on each other to keep warm. I don't remember how long it took to get out of the mountains, but I counted twenty-seven tunnels. When the train stopped somewhere east of Sacramento, we were coal black, smelled like urine, and hadn't eaten in three days.

We switched to a boxcar with four or five blacks. An older black man took pity on us, "You boys like an orange? Here, take the whole bag." We ate peelings and all, and then proceeded to wretch and wretch, adding the smell of vomit to our already indescribable stench. An old man patted me on the back, "You're gonna be alright, boy. Just you hang on. You're gonna be alright. You just stick with old Jake and I'll get you to Frisco."

When we rolled into San Francisco, Bob refused to jump off the train. He'd had a knee operation a few weeks before we left Vale and his knee was not looking too good. The hitchhiking had aggravated it and the constant jarring of the first train car left him in constant pain. He figured he would be going back to the hospital if he slipped and fell. Laverne and I jumped, but Bob clung to the door of the freight car. We ran beside the train, urging him to jump before it picked up too much speed. He finally lay on his back, held his knee to his chest, and rolled out the door. His knee survived, but his left shoulder didn't fare too well.

We had arrived, as dirty as the three little pigs, as smelly as a ship's head, and as bruised as three drunks in a brawl. To cap it off, we didn't have a dime to make a call to Bob's aunt and uncle. No one would help us, wouldn't even come near us. We convinced a policeman to lend us a dime. He insisted on listening to the call and wanted his dime back when our ride came. Tim and Billy had ratted on us, so the Radissons had been expecting us for a couple days. They were good Catholics who believed it was their Christian duty to feed and clothe the hungry. I have no doubt they received an extra indulgence for looking after us. When we reached their house, two showers and a bath were waiting. Once cleaned up, we sat down to a chicken dinner with mashed potatoes and gravy, and all the trimmings. This time we eased into the eating and came back later for the pie and ice cream. Mrs. Radisson made us feel like heroes for having made it all the way to San Francisco.

Dad and Mr. Clauson were already on their way from Oregon to pick us up. I was preparing myself for the wrath of Roth but got quite a surprise. Dad had driven to California many times doing fruit and produce runs. Not wanting to waste a good trip, he wanted to look up his old friends in Chinatown and show us the sights. We rode the cable cars, saw the Golden Gate Bridge, explored the shipyards, and gazed across at Alcatraz Island. The trolley took us to Playland, an amusement park that covered ten acres and was located next to Ocean Beach. The Big Dipper rollercoaster and the Whip airplane swing made the little fairs that visited Vale and Ontario seem like children's playgrounds. There were shooting galleries, baseball throws, a massive Ferris wheel, and a first-rate carousel. That's one trip I will never forget.

Remember Rudy and Johnny, our two "buddies" who left us in the brush and waved from the back of a truck? The truck was in an accident. When we returned, Rudy's arm was in a cast and Johnny was still in the hospital. With what happened to Rudy and Johnny, and hearing of our ordeal riding the rails, our high school principal decided we should address the school in an assembly with a theme along the lines of "The Perils of Running Away." During the presentation, our suffering and misery somehow transformed into a tale of heroic survival and adventure. "California was better than we could ever have imagined. It had been the experience of..." The principal ended the assembly midway for fear other students might catch the next freight headed south.

Just as I was settling back into my routine of school, baseball, and weekends at the barbershop, Principal Higgins dropped by the house to confront my dad. He held out a draft notice that Mom had forwarded to the school. The principal accused Dad of lying about my age to keep me out of the army. According to the draft notice, I was twenty years old. Dad cleared up the misunderstanding with the principal, but told him, "Let him think he's drafted. He needs to learn a lesson." That backfired. I was ready to leave. When the truth came out, I reluctantly surrendered my treasured draft card.

I might have known that Mom had ulterior motives. Two days later, I received a letter which stated in part, "Lee and I are in a little trouble. We need you to come home and help us get out of the hole." She wanted me to quit school, take a job in Milton-Freewater, Oregon, and help support her and her husband. When I told Dad, he was furious. He phoned Mom and they had a fiery argument. It was one of the few times I remember Dad standing up for me.

From the time I was about six years old, I had been contributing most of the money I earned directly to Mom. I had already been cheated by Lee time and again. Seemed to me that he should be supporting the family. I didn't want to join them. I was finishing the best year I ever had in high school. I had a shoeshine stand that brought me more money than my buddies were making doing farm work. I was living with Dad and his second wife, Dorothy. I was experiencing the closest thing I would ever have to a real family. Just thinking about living with Mom and Lee put me into a state of resentment and depression. When would it be my turn to be happy? I wanted to stay with Dad but felt obligated to Mom. It wasn't fair to expect me to choose one parent over the other. I thought, "You two can go straight to hell! I'm going to get married and have my own wife and family. You can all just go to hell!"

I had been going steady with a girl named Wanda Burt. I liked her family and they liked me. If I could convince Wanda, and more importantly her dad, we could get married and leave my crazy family behind. I stalked out the front door and headed for town. I was cutting across the park in downtown Vale when I came across a little freshman named Betty Allen. Her family had been part of the mass migration of poor farmers leaving the fields of Texas and Oklahoma for the orchards of California in the late 1930s. From there, the Allens had come north into Oregon. I didn't even know her name but there she was, sitting on the grass with her back against a tree crying.

I asked, "Are you okay?"

"My daddy's dying and my boyfriend from Weiser jilted me and what's more, I think I'm pregnant." She then burst into uncontrollable sobbing.

"You want to get married?"

"Okay."

Chapter Notes

[1]A couple years later, Gary's buddy, Buzz Boemer joined the Navy. Buzz's first voyage was to Hawaii. He spent the whole trip over and back in the sickbay struggling with seasickness. Then he received a medical discharge. The Navy isn't for everyone.

PRICKLY PEAR

TWO PLANTS PRODUCE beautiful yellow flowers in Texas, roses and prickly pear cactus. When I met Betty Jean Allen with her sweet southern drawl, I thought I had found "The Yellow Rose of Texas," but looking back, I think she was more like a little prickly pear in bloom. Roses have thorns and prickly pear have spines, so either one needs to be handled with care.

The earliest accounts of Betty's family go back to the American Civil War. While her Great Grandpa Allen was languishing and soon to die in a Yankee prison camp, William Tecumseh Sherman was destroying everything in sight in his infamous march to the sea. Sherman summarized his scorched earth policy by saying, "If a crow flies over this route, it will have to carry its own rations." Sherman was determined that the South would never rise again. By the time he crossed Betty's Great Grandpa McCracken's plantation, the McCrackens had hidden their home-cured meats and root vegetables in random pits scattered throughout their fields. The family survived, but like many others, was impoverished by the war's end. Meanwhile, General Benjamin Franklin Terry[1], a distant cousin-to-be, was killed while leading the 8th Texas Calvary, known as Terry's Texas Rangers. So, there I was, a young man with Union supporters on my mom's side of the family and Mennonite pacifists on my dad's side, about to marry a girl with a bloodline of strong southern pride. I might have known that one day we would have our own "civil" war.

One of the McCracken daughters, Luquincy Elizabeth, married James Otwell[2] on July 19th, 1874. With little to look forward to in their home state of Georgia, they joined a wagon train with five other families and made the three-month trek to Texas in search of free land and a new life. Old family stories tell of the women washing clothes with homemade lye soap and hanging them on the brush surrounding the water holes. Cows were milked and the butter was churned with the jostling of the wagons. In Texas, the Otwells settled alongside the Terrys of Comanche County. One of the daughters, Mittie Otwell, married George Terry. Their daughter, Faye Alice Terry, married Elbert Cheatham Allen. It was their middle daughter, Betty Jean, who became my wife.

When we married, Betty's family was only a little more than two generations from having been slave owners and staunch defenders of the Confederacy. After the war, they reluctantly admitted that slavery was wrong, but like many southerners, felt a need to defend how they had treated their slaves. Faye several times told the story of an uncle riding all night to corroborate the alibi of a black man about to be hung for stealing a cow. "Right is right and wrong is wrong, and no man's wrong is right," summed up her belief. She had a good Methodist upbringing. In her mind, saving the man was the godly thing to do. In the uncle's mind, it may have been simple economics. A good slave was worth a lot of money.

Dovie *Otwell* Nabors, when interviewed by the *Comanche Chief* newspaper in 1979 said, "Both of my grandparents, the McCrackens and the Otwells, owned slaves. They were good to their slaves; they fed them; they never did whip or abuse them. And on selling day when slaves were to be sold, they wouldn't divide man and wife or children." Many other stories were passed on about the slave days and I don't doubt these had their impact on Betty's outlook. Commenting on *Uncle Tom's Cabin,* Dovie said, "I found [a lot] was true as to the things [my parents] said about *other* slave owners, that they were mean to their slaves...." She continued with the account of a black man bringing a baby to the Otwell's shortly after the war. His wife was seriously ill, and he needed someone to care for the child until she recovered. James and Luquincy took the baby and cared for it like it was their own. Weeks went by and the neighbors began wagging their heads. James simply told people, "I believe the man's story and in time this baby will be returned to its family." After several months the man returned for his baby.

Betty must have been the queen of sarcasm. She shut down more than one racist conversation with, "Oh yeah...we treated our slaves good." Her point being that slavery, even if compassionately practiced, is still slavery. She had no place for prejudice of any kind in our home[3], and I believe she was one of the most compassionate people I've ever known when it came to concern for the disadvantaged.

Betty's Grandma Mittie passed on a couple stories that fueled the imaginations of her young granddaughters. Around 1900, Mittie and Grandpa George lived on a farm in Stonewall County about twelve miles from the nearest town, Aspermont. Like other farmers in Central Texas, the Terrys found themselves in the midst of a range war. Ranchers wanted open range for their cattle and free access to water. Farmers insisted on fences to protect their crops and water rights. Every morning, George rode around his homestead driving stray cattle out of his fields and repairing damaged fence lines. Every night, local cattlemen tore down more sections of fence, hoping to drive the Terrys off the land.

In exasperation, George hired a young man named Jim Nolan to ride fences so George could get on with the business of farming. Jim and his young pregnant wife were given the upstairs of the Terry's home. It happened that early one morning while George was on his way to Aspermont for supplies and Jim was riding fence, Mittie heard a gunshot. She asked Jim's wife to stay in the house with the Terry children while Mittie went to investigate. As she rode her horse toward the stock pond, she saw several men dragging Jim's body through the grass. The men broke and ran. Mittie turned and rode for help. When the neighbors arrived at the scene, the killers had returned and were about to drop the body into the pond. Once again, they dropped Jim, mounted their horses, and fled.

The night after Jim's burial, Mittie was wakened by sounds coming from the upstairs. She heard someone getting out of bed, taking time to dress, and slowly walking down the stairs. Mittie peeked out her bedroom door and saw a man with a large black hat pulled low over his forehead. He then descended the stairs and vanished through the front door. The following night Mittie stood at the foot of the stairs with a shotgun raised to stop the shadowy figure. The ghostly form glided through the barrel and disappeared into the night.

Jim Nolan's mother heard the story and asked if she could sleep in Jim's room. The following morning, with tears in her eyes and a tremor in her voice, she claimed she had seen the ghost of her son. George and Mittie begged her not to tell anyone. They were determined to move out and didn't want stories of a haunted house to block the sale. In rural Texas it was common for travelers to ask local farmers for lodging. Before long an elderly man who was driving cattle to Aspermont asked to spend the night. He had heard about the ghost of Jim Nolan and wanted to spend a night in Jim's old room. The following morning at breakfast he said, "Well, I am an old man and I have never seen or heard anything like that!" Just to be certain the apparition was not the product of grief and imagination, Mittie lodged several more travelers in the same room over the following weeks. All claimed to see a ghost and the most common comment was, "You may live here if you like, but we would not be here when the sun goes down!" In time the land sold, but the new owner tore the house down. This story was passed down by Mittie to her grandson, Fred Nabors. She concluded her account, "Perhaps [Jim] Nolan can sleep the long sleep now and not have to make his nightly rounds."

The ghost of Jim Nolan was not the only story of the "other side" that circulated in the Terry family. One of Betty's aunts, Minnie is the name I recall, was overburdened with work and children. It seemed her husband only came around long enough to get her pregnant and then disappeared for the next ten to twelve months before repeating the cycle. Minnie went into a state of despair while striving to look after the home place and provide for her children. While struggling through her eighth or ninth pregnancy, she decided better to lose the baby than add another hungry mouth to the family. Minnie began praying that God would take the baby. She claimed that on the night she went into labor, the Death Angel appeared at the foot of her bed and took the baby's soul, leaving only a lifeless stillborn.

Betty's mother, Faye, was born August 25th, 1911, the sixth of seven children. Her folks had six girls. There was also a little boy, Elmer, who died during his first year. The Texas Range Wars were over, but World War I soon commenced, followed by the Spanish Flu, The Great Depression, and the Dirty Thirties, enough hard times to test the mettle of everybody. On entering her teens, Faye went to work in a laundry to help support the family. West Texas is hot, and the old laundries were even hotter. She often suffered from the heat and recounted stepping out of the laundry, vomiting behind the building, and then returning to work. She did whatever was needed to help her family and showed the same loyalty and sacrifice to her children years later.

Hard times and a Methodist upbringing make for a somewhat dry sense of humor. Once, she assured one of the grandkids that they had rich relatives in Texas. Why, one of the uncles "had so many goats, he couldn't count them." Of course, the kids, having no understanding of wealth or sarcasm, thought they really did have rich relatives somewhere in Texas. Another time, she was explaining to Terry, one of her grandsons, how to make a trot line. Terry had a worried look on his face and said, "But Grandma, trot lines are against the law."

"Don't matter," she replied. "In Texas everyone owns their own river."

Elbert Cheatham Allen, known simply as Eb, was a character fit for a Charles Dickens novel. Whereas Faye believed "God will look after us," Eb was more, "Do unto others before they do it unto you." It seems he was a man who lived for the moment. Betty told the story of her dad as a teenager impulsively spending his summer earnings on a tow bag (burlap bag) filled with fireworks rather than giving the money to his mother. When his father found out, he took the bag into the front yard and lit it on fire. A summer's earnings went up in flames in less than ten minutes.

I don't know how Eb and Faye met or any details of their marriage, but they were a striking couple. They happened to be making a road trip while another "striking" couple from Texas, Clyde Barrow and Bonnie Parker, were making their own road trip across parts of Texas, Oklahoma, and Missouri. Before Bonnie and Clyde parked their 1934

Ford Fordor Deluxe for the last time, nine police officers and several civilians who got in their way had died. So, what do you do when you come across a young woman standing next to a Ford sedan with a flat tire on an isolated stretch of Texas highway? On the other hand, what do you do if you're a young woman stuck on the side of the road and a young couple pulls up beside your car?

Stopping to help was the Good Samaritan thing to do, not to mention that Eb had an eye for attractive women. So as Eb and Faye pulled beside the other car, Eb said in a loud voice, "You keep the gun on her and if anyone jumps out of the brush, shoot!" He then stepped out and proceeded to change the tire. When he finished, he made the woman get in her car and drive ahead of them until they were out of the area. Of course, there was no gun and Faye probably wouldn't have pulled the trigger anyway. Eb was a master when it came to a con or a bluff.

By the mid-thirties Faye had given birth to three daughters, Nancy, Betty, and Patsy. Times were hard and getting harder and people coped in different ways. Faye found strength in her faith. Eb found strength in the bottle. One afternoon, the three girls came across Eb's stash of whiskey. They decided that the best thing to do was to pour out the whiskey and break the bottles. When Eb found the broken bottles, he went into a rage. Each of the girls was given a severe beating. There wasn't much Faye could do. In the 1930s a man was king of his castle; divorce was unheard of; and a woman could expect little support outside of the home. The girls had welts and lacerations on their thighs and legs. Faye doctored them the best she knew. Then she brought out their long church dresses. These would have to do for a week or so. It wouldn't do for anyone to see their battered little legs.

The family settled in San Angelo in west-central Texas. It was known for its cattle, sheep, and goats. The

Allens didn't have cattle, sheep, or goats. Times were bum and getting bummer. According to Betty, folks down the road were eating the neighborhood cats. When Eb found what he thought to be a dog tooth in a tamale, he decided it was time to hit the highway along with other poor Texans and the masses of Okies headed for California. He traded their car and what little they had for a 1933 Ford flatbed truck and built a small canvas-roofed shack on the back, his own rendition of a truck camper. At least they would have a place to sleep at night. There was plenty of room outdoors for cooking and other domestic needs. Some folks warned that California was just "pie in the sky," but Eb reasoned it had to be better than West Texas and it certainly couldn't be worse. Of course, nothing ever goes as planned.

Faye had a friend named Charlene. Charlene's husband had deserted her, leaving his wife and two little girls destitute. Charlene dropped by the Allen's to say goodbye. It's not hard to imagine the two women having a prayer and a cry. Faye muttered, "I wish you were going with us." Charlene quickly responded, "I think I will. I'll get packed right now." As the account goes, Eb was beside himself. Faye reminded him that it was the Christian thing to do and Eb couldn't say no.

The most direct route from San Angelo to California was via Highway 10 through Phoenix and then cross-country to California. Relatives in California would be waiting. The last stop before California was Ehrenberg, Arizona. It had been a steamboat stop on the Colorado River but, with the coming of the railroad, wasn't much more than a trailer park town by the 1930s. The Allens likely joined other migrants at a campground beside the Colorado River. That night they experienced the vengeance of Arizona mosquitoes. Exposed body parts of the three adults and five little girls were covered in bites. The mosquitoes were so thick there seemed to be bites on top of bites. Nancy, Betty, and Patsy scratched until they bled. The following day they were turned back at the California border. The border guard was convinced the girls had a communicable disease. It might be some form of chicken pox or measles or who knows what, but whatever it was, it was not coming into California. That meant returning to Ehrenberg, and knowing Eb, a probable late-night border crossing while the children were "asleep".

Eb's California relatives took the family right in. Nothing like southern hospitality. The first morning they went all out: bacon and eggs, pancakes, oatmeal, a regular menu. Eb asked Betty, "What do you want for breakfast? You can have whatever you want."

"Could I have some beans?"

"Sorry honey, they don't have beans. What else would you like?"

"Well then, is there any of the juice left?"

Pretty sad, when a good meal in a little girl's mind is a bowl of beans. Life could only get better once Eb went to work and there were plenty of opportunities in the fields and vineyards of California.

You've probably heard the 1956 song "With a Little Bit of Luck" written for the play *My Fair Lady*. It could have been Eb Allen's theme song, though apart from the verse about liquor, "with a little bit of luck you'll give right in," most of the time luck never came his way. Another part of the song goes, "with a little bit of luck, when your neighbor comes 'round you won't be home!" They weren't settled in California long before the Johnsons, relatives from Texas, came calling. "Do unto others as they do unto you," was just fine. Problem with these folks, they were content to just stay. So, how do you ask "family" to leave? Eb wanted to just give them a good Texas boot and say "GIT!" Faye insisted that it just wouldn't be Christian. Her belief was found in the same song, "The Lord above made man to help his neighbor."

One evening Eb came home from work to find the icebox filled with bacon, a nice pork roast, and a couple steaks. A big bag of potatoes had been placed in the corner of the kitchen. Fresh fruit was on the table. His normal semi-frown turned to a big smile. Maybe it wouldn't be so bad having the Johnsons stay on. After all, two families can do right well if they share expenses. That week they had the finest feeds since leaving Texas and no "dog tooth" in the tamale.

When Eb found out the food had been put on his tab at the local store, he went apoplectic. Fortunately for the Johnsons, they weren't at home when he confronted Faye. Once again, she played the "good Lord" card and added the "family" card to make a pair. Come evening the two families sat down to a more traditional meal of cornbread and beans. Eb mentioned he had been to the store, but before he brought up the bill, he began clutching his chest and fell off his chair. He quickly dispatched Betty to fetch the doctor. Faye was scared out of her wits. She knew Eb had the occasional heart palpitation but was totally unaware that he had been seeing a doctor. She helped Eb into the bedroom and waited. About forty minutes later, a man in an unkempt suit and grey hat, carrying a weather-beaten medical bag, came rushing into the house. The doctor attended Eb for about twenty minutes before coming out of the bedroom. He said that Eb had suffered a heart attack and enquired about the crowded living conditions. Complete peace and quiet was needed if Eb was going to make it. His own private room was a necessity. It was agreed that the Johnsons would have to leave. Eb told them how "sorry" he was and how much he would miss them, but what can a man with a heart condition do? By this point, Faye recognized that the "doctor" was one of Eb's drinking buddies.

The day after the Johnsons left, Eb had a full recovery. He did have a heart condition. How could it be otherwise? He was a heavy drinker. He smoked both cigarettes and a pipe. He sniffed and chewed tobacco to the extent that paint was coming off the side of his truck where he spit out the window. Eventually his heart would be his demise, but for the time being life was back to normal. Things weren't all that was promised in California. One day Eb came home and told Faye to pack the truck. He'd decided to move the family to the small country town of Vale, Oregon.

Chapter Notes

[1]Benjamin Franklin Terry is not in Betty's direct lineage.

[2]This information is from an article passed to Betty, "Wagon Wheels keep on turnin'" in the *Commanche Chief* newspaper, November 1st, 1979. James and Luquincy Otwell parented eleven children: Claude, Marvin, Rufus, Susie, Effie, Willie, Lovie, Jack, Dovie, Mittie, and Minnie. Mittie was Betty's grandmother.

[3]When Gary wanted to join the Independent Order of Odd Fellows, which barred blacks from membership, Betty was adamant, "No husband of mine will ever join a racist club." In 1971, the IOOF changed its constitution, removing the whites only clause.

Betty's Father – Elbert Cheatham Allen

Betty's Mother – Faye Terry Allen

California here we come! Faye is standing on right. Betty is second child from left.

Betty in Center

Circa 1947

Betty on Right - Age 13

PURPLE PASSION

I WAS CUTTING ACROSS the park in downtown Vale when I came across a little freshman named Betty Allen. I didn't even know her name but there she was, sitting on the grass with her back against a tree crying. I asked, "Are you okay?"

"My daddy's dying and my boyfriend from Weiser jilted me and what's more, I think I'm pregnant."

"You want to get married?"

"Okay."

How stupid can two people get? I was seventeen years old and Betty was fourteen. That evening, I broke the news to Dad while helping muck out the barn. For a moment I thought he had gone catatonic. He held his breath and stared at his shovel blade. Then he looked me in the eyes and said, "You walk out that gate and I'll lay this shovel right between your shoulders." Dad was never one to show mercy, whether it was wrestling, chores, or whatever. I turned around and walked out, hoping he would stop me and bracing myself for the impact. How I wish he would have kept his word. Years later I asked him why he didn't. He answered, "I was afraid I might kill you."

Three days later, while walking home from school, an old DeSoto sedan pulled up beside me. The driver reached over and pushed the passenger door open. Eb Allen, Betty's father, leveled a shotgun at me and said, "Get in the car." We drove about a mile out of town and pulled off the road.

"I hear you're gonna marry my daughter."

"Yes sir, I am."

"Well, are you gonna take good care of her?"

"I wouldn't marry her if I couldn't take care of her."

"You better." Eb did a U-turn and drove back to town. "Now, get out."

I decided to settle my affairs, such as they were. I figured I could take the job at Milton-Freewater. I just wouldn't send Mom any of my pay. No one would buy my car, a 1936 Pontiac. I had paid the Ford dealership in Ontario $250 for it, but never managed to get the title. Instead of helping me deal with the company, Dad had said, "Next time you'll know better than to pay for something without a clear title." The wrecking yard was willing to take it for a parts car and gave me $45. My shoeshine stand had been earning 14-15 dollars a week. With what I got from the car and what I had been saving, I had over $140 but I felt guilty about not helping Mom, so I sent her the money. My Navy experience taught me that Mom had a way of interfering in my plans and I wanted her to think I was already married, so I wrote this letter[1]:

Dear Mom,

Well, I got your letter. It kind of left me up in the air. If something [is] wrong, I sure want you to tell me. Dad didn't know quite what to say either. I don't quite know what you meant when you told Dad that I needed to settle down. By the way, I'm going to have to. Maybe you had better sit down before you read this next line. Mom, I'm married. I married Miss Betty Allen here of Vale. I really do love her, Mother. We've been married a week now. Dad doesn't know, but I'm going to tell [him soon].

Betty is really a nice girl. She says she would like to come over and see you and if it is possible that I can get a job we may stay. I've told her a lot about you and she really thinks she'll like you. Well, if you've gotten over it, now you can get up. We may be over within the next two weeks. Please write and tell me what to expect when we get there. And Mom, this is the first thing I've really been satisfied with.

We both want to leave Vale. Her mother knows about it and, of course, she says we are too young, but Mom, I'll never find another girl like her. She is now Mrs. Betty Jean Roth and I love her. I suppose this is kind of a shock to you but I'm always shocking someone. Please don't tell Lee or Sally until we get over there.

Well, don't you write and blame Dad, because he doesn't even know. I should [tell him but] I'm kind of taking my time about it, [waiting] for a chance.

Dorothy is home and fine. It sure is a cute little kid she has. Grandmother, Dad, and Sandy are fine too. Whatever you do, Mom, don't get mad. You'll see why I did it when I get over there. Please write and tell me more about your summer plans. Will try to make it over in about two weeks. I'll bring Betty along, so be expecting her. Please write back and give me hell before I get over there because it might hurt Betty's feelings.

All the love I've got left over,
Gary

We ran into roadblocks right away. Pastor Cecil Hannon of the Methodist Church in Payette was willing to perform the ceremony, but the age of consent in Idaho was eighteen. I was seventeen and Betty was only fourteen. With parental consent, a sixteen- or seventeen-year-old could marry, but Betty would have needed a court order stating exceptional circumstances. Faye, Betty's mother, was beside herself with the thought of Betty being pregnant. Pregnant teenage girls in the 1940s were sent to "visit an aunt" before the pregnancy showed and returned several months later as though nothing had happened. At the same time, Eb had been readmitted to the hospital and given only weeks to live. Faye didn't know what would become of her and her three daughters, and she wanted to do the "right thing." Dad shared her conviction and agreed to sign for me. Reluctantly, Faye signed a marriage license stating that Betty was sixteen. We tied the knot May 19, 1949. Incidentally, Betty may have missed a period, but she was not pregnant.

The evening of the wedding I didn't have $2.00 to pay Pastor Hannon, but I reasoned it was better to owe than stop the show. I could look after him later. Few people will believe that Betty and I had only kissed two or three times. We spent our wedding night with our respective parents.

We met at the hospital the following morning to say goodbye to Betty's dad. Eb was relieved to know that Betty would be looked after. He realized how badly I needed the job in Milton-Freewater and insisted we be on our way. It was an emotional farewell with no guarantee of ever seeing him again.

Dad was waiting outside the hospital. He kept saying, "You better buy your tickets." I didn't have a dime and was too proud to admit it. Even Betty didn't know that I didn't have any money. She kept fidgeting with a little ball of paper about the size of a marble. It slipped out of her hand and I picked it up. It was a twenty-dollar bill that Eb had slipped into her pocket. It was not enough to get us to Milton-Freewater, but it would get us to Pendleton, Oregon, only thirty-five miles short of our destination. We boarded the bus, a seventeen-year-old boy with his fourteen-year-old bride and were on our way.

Pendleton was a classic "cow town growed big." It sported the Pendleton Stampede, one of the largest rodeos in the western United States; had a Chinatown going back to the rail construction of the 1800s; and was home to a state mental hospital. A few airmen were still around from an air base that had been used for training pilots during World War II. I stepped off the bus with a grand total of one dollar and forty cents in my pocket, just enough for a snack between us. It was too late to start hitchhiking, so we walked to the Temple Hotel across the street from the bus depot. I approached the front desk and asked if we could sit in the lobby until morning. As I explained our plight, a voice came from the stairwell, "You kids running away, or are you really married?" A railroad engineer walked down the stairs. He told the front desk, "Send the maid up to my room. I'll be gone for four days. Let these kids use the room and give them anything they need, a wedding present from me." We stayed two days while I earned a few dollars cleaning the hotel grounds. As soon as I had enough money, I bought bus tickets to Milton-Freewater.

The cannery in Milton-Freewater put me right to work. A small abandoned house stood on the hill just across from the cannery. I tracked down the owner. He was willing to give us two months of free rent for cleaning up the grounds and painting the house. All the moves I had made with my mom had taught me a thing or two about how to make do.

We weren't there long when Betty's sister, Nancy, showed up with her boyfriend, Dale Barnes. Betty was only four foot eleven, just a tiny little thing, but she was a firecracker. She wanted to shoot Dale because he and Nancy weren't married. No one was going to take advantage of her sister. It took some convincing to assure her that Dale's intentions were good.

The peak season for cherries, plums, and asparagus had just passed, so Dale and I went to work on a pea vining crew and were soon working sixteen-hour days. Betty and Nancy kept busy cleaning, painting, and fixing the house. We were four teenagers having a grand adventure. Coming off a night shift for our first day off in two weeks, Dale and I went for haircuts. I had been trying to grow out a Mohawk and wanted something clean and stylish, like the styles worn by Gary Cooper and John Wayne. You know, parted on the side, combed over, and swept back. There was only one barber, but the shop had two chairs. Dale went first while I waited in the second chair. Within seconds, I was dead asleep. The barber finished with Dale but was unable to rouse me. He asked Dale, "What does he want?"

"Oh, he just wants it shaved." I could have killed Dale.

The canning season finished at the end of September and we headed back to Payette in a 1932 Hudson. The tires had dry rot and we didn't get far before our first flat tire. We didn't have a jack, but I did have a tire patch kit. We waved a passing car down and borrowed a jack. Three flat tires later we were stranded on a deserted stretch of highway hoping to flag down yet another passing car. It was getting dark, so we took our bedding into a nearby barn for the night.

We woke up to a big commotion in the barnyard corrals. Cows were bellowing. Calves were bawling. The clip-clop of horses and occasional "whoa, easy now" echoed through the loft hole. A local ranch was bringing in a herd of cattle for shipment to Pendleton. Three big cowboys offered to help us. They simply lifted the rear corner of the Hudson onto a block so I could change the tire and then lifted it off when I finished. It's a good thing Betty and Nancy were there. I doubt those cowboys would have done it for me and Dale. For lack of material, I used an old *Sears* catalogue as a "boot" to protect the inner tube from the holes in the tire. Later, when I replaced the tire, I found that the pages of the catalogue had come loose and were fanned out around the entire inside of the tire[2].

Arriving at Payette, Betty and I spent the first two weeks at Leonard and Jeanne's. My back was killing me, and I just couldn't figure out why. Leonard took me aside and suggested that we try separate beds for a while. It might be good to give both of us a rest. Problem solved.

If you're not picky, there is always work to be found. I was soon working as a baker's helper and we moved into a tiny two-room house. I hadn't yet turned eighteen. Betty was fifteen years old and six months pregnant. We thought we were pretty grown up. *Did we ever have a lot to learn!* Thankfully, my mother was there to help when Betty came due. Mom had also given birth at age fifteen and was well aware of the role ignorance plays when it comes to sex and pregnancy. We didn't talk about it, but she made sure our babies were born in the hospital.

It was a hard labor and the baby just wouldn't come. Betty was so small, and Terry was seven pounds, eight ounces. Dr. Kotas had resorted to the dreaded forceps to drag the poor little guy into this world. Terry's head was so bruised and marked that when they presented him to Betty, she refused to accept him. He was not the beautiful little baby she had been expecting and couldn't possibly be hers. It took three days of convincing by which time Terry looked a lot better. In 1950, dads were not allowed in the delivery room. My role was to strut around handing out cigars, a role which I did very well.

The baby cried all the time. Betty didn't have sufficient milk to feed Terry and he was allergic to cow's milk, so I bought a goat. He was keeping his food down, but he still cried and cried. Mom recognized the problem right away. The little guy was cold. His little cotton infant blanket would have been fine in June, but this was February. The only heat in our house came from a small oil stove in the living room.

We were so dumb when it came to babies. It didn't cross our minds that diapers could be washed and reused. We were using any piece of cloth we could find and then throwing the dirties down the privy. Mom caught me about to dump a bucket full of diapers and put a stop to that. It was too cold to hang them outside to dry, so we ran a clothesline through the living room.

That was a cold winter followed by a late spring. The fruit trees were just budding when a severe frost descended on Payette. I went out at 5:00 in the morning to help smudge[3]. When I came in, I filled the oil stove before returning to bed. About an hour later Betty woke up. Smoke was wafting through the cracks of our bedroom door. The living room was ablaze. Our room had no window, so we wrapped the baby and ourselves in a large blanket and made a run through the living room. The blanket caught fire, but we got out. Betty was in her nightgown, Terry was wrapped in a crib blanket, and I was in my pajamas. By the time the volunteer fire department arrived, only one wall was standing. There was little they could do. I convinced them to push the standing wall into the fire so the clean-up would be easier. The fire chief determined that someone had mixed gasoline with the oil to enhance the smudging. It was a deadly mixture in our little stove.

Just before the fire, I was given more responsibility at the bakery. I was learning to make cream puffs, Danishes, and bear claws. My weakness for milk and donuts probably goes back to the fresh-baked cinnamon rolls and donuts. I was yet to learn the art of making cakes, but more than willing to help with quality control. Part of the job required knowing the different recipes, so I had taken the master recipe book home. The book was destroyed in the fire and I was "fired" for having taken company property. As the embers cooled, we found ourselves with no home, no possessions, and no job.

I soon got on with Guernsey Gold Dairy. All the small farms around Payette and Ontario kept at least two or three milk cows. My job was picking up cans of fresh milk. Just about every farmer had one to five cans at the entry to his lane ready for pick-up every morning. The monthly cream check kept many of those small farms operating. The little milk truck had a single stool-style seat for the driver and open doors on both sides. As soon as Terry was walking, I occasionally took him along. Since there was no seat for him, he sat in an old-fashioned Borden's Milk box.

While with Guernsey Gold, Dad came to spend a couple weeks with Betty and me. He was out of work and insisted on helping with my milk route. I thought he just wanted to go along for company but come payday he asked for half the check. Said he had earned it. It's hard to stand up to your own dad, but I had a wife and child plus we had been feeding him. I made just enough to pay our bills and put food on the table. Mooching off family members was something Dad had done off and on for most of his life. Whenever he was out of work, he would head for the home of one relative or another. He had overstayed his welcome with everyone else and could now add me to the list. I loved my Dad and he was fun to be around, but there was another side to him.

In the meantime, I had located a forty by twenty-foot building sitting in a field on the edge of town. The locals claimed it was haunted. One story was that a calf had been found in it that was frozen solid standing in an upright position. That seemed explainable, but people also said they heard voices and saw dim figures going through the building late at night. I didn't believe a word, but the owner, Blair Scott told me, "If you can move it, it's yours!" The building had no foundation and would have been easy to move except for one problem, a ten-foot wide by six-foot deep ditch that circled the property. It was too good a deal to pass up and I've always believed, "Where there's a will, there's a way."

Lee had a friend that owned a Cat Excavator and the necessary cables to pull the building. Poles, borrowed from the local power company, served as interchangeable rollers to convey the building across the field. Additional poles were used as a temporary bridge across the canal. It required quite a balancing act, but we had our house. I soon divided the building into three rooms, a bedroom, a living room, and a kitchen. We still had the privy from the previous house and thought we were set, but not for long. The doors began opening and closing in the middle of the night. Anytime Betty passed near me an invisible force shoved me against the wall. We moved!

When you think of a married couple with one child, generally you don't picture an eighteen-year-old boy and a fifteen-year-old girl. I always had a job which meant a place to go and people to see every day. Poor Betty was stuck at home with a toddler and nowhere to go.

Terry could be a regular little turd bird[4]. The little shit kept sneaking off to the local service station. The hoist fascinated him, and the mechanics obligingly ran it up and down, knowing that Betty would be there within minutes. They thought it so funny to see her switch his little behind all the way home, knowing the little rascal would be back in an hour or so. Terry one time licked and pasted a page of postage stamps on our fishbowl. When asked how the stamps got there, he said he didn't know, "Maybe Daddy did it." In the 1950s, a teenager with a child would never be allowed to attend school, let alone a married woman. Even the local pool would have considered Betty a bad influence on the summer swim and dive team. Betty was not to be deterred. She began telling people that Terry was her little brother, that she had to babysit him while her parents worked. I have to say, she had a great figure and was excellent both on the diving board and in the water. She wouldn't have many summers to enjoy. She was pregnant and having babies for most of the next ten years.

Weekends were for partying and we wanted to be in the action, hence the invention of "purple passion." Purple passion was a mixture of one gallon of grape juice to one fifth of vodka. We couldn't buy or drink alcohol at the local dances, but the occasional trip to the car was all we needed. After a couple glasses of purple passion, if anyone gave Betty a "come on" look, the fight was on. Dark green may be the color for jealousy, but purple was close enough. Betty loved being fought over, and she loved watching me fight. A circle would form, and she would cheer as if we were at a boxing match.

Whenever I was getting beat up, she jumped in to help. I remember a big guy taking me down in a parking lot. I had rolled, and my head slid under a car bumper. Every time I tried to raise up, I banged my forehead on the bottom of the bumper. Blood was everywhere! Every time the fellow straddling me tried to punch me in the face, he smashed his knuckles on the top edge of the bumper. More blood! Betty jumped on his back with her legs wrapped around his body and her hands jerking his head back. She was a wild one. That bumper saved me from a real beating. Someone yelled that the cops were coming and everyone jumped in their cars and peeled out of the parking lot. Betty held her alcohol far better than me. How many mornings I remember seeing the color purple swirling down the toilet.

When the Carnation Milk Company in Ontario offered me a job driving their large tank trucks, I gladly made the move. Western Idaho and eastern Oregon were renowned in the 1950s for pheasant hunting. Pheasants were seen in the fields in the evenings and could be flushed from the ditches and fence lines almost everywhere. Because they are birds that generally run instead of fly, there were always dead birds along the highway. On my way out of Ontario with the tanker truck I always took note of birds that had been killed the previous day. On my return trip, I picked up any fresh kills that occurred while I was running my route. There was no point in wasting good meat, and fried pheasant is delicious.

I was working at Carnation when I finally had my shoulder operated on. It was getting so bad that anytime I reached backward I was taking a chance of dislocating it. That and constant pain made surgery a necessity. In surgery, the doctor drilled a hole through the ball of my upper arm, ran a ligament through the hole, and then attached it to the shoulder. The operation shifted the muscle configuration somewhat. There is no longer any muscle under my right arm. The surgery was relatively new, and the results were sketchy. For many men, the motion in the affected shoulder was so limited that the arm gradually atrophied and became not much more than an oversized chicken wing. Carnation was good to me. They put me on light duty, spraying out the milk cans that came through every day. I could do the job with one arm, but my right arm began to shrink and contract. I decided to push through the pain and put it to work.

The stainless-steel lid for a milk can weighs about three pounds. The lids were stacked on a rack at about shoulder height, a good foot higher than my reach with that arm. I started holding a lid in my right hand, throwing my arm up to mid-waist level, and flipping the lid onto the rack. It took a little practice, but my arm began to recover its strength and the ligaments gradually stretched to where I could reach the rack. That arm is still slightly limited compared to my left arm, but you would have to have a good eye to tell. The arm was barely mended when I fell from the side of a large milk tank and broke my back. What an ordeal! I spent weeks in the hospital in traction, finally had several discs fused together, and then spent several more weeks in a three-quarter body cast.

The local owner of the Carnation Company, Bob Wolfe, had a hard life. He accidentally lost his left leg in a hunting accident. One of his two sons was killed by a train just a few weeks after his daughter-in-law had committed suicide. The other son, Ted, was hell-bent. Ted was giving me a ride to work in his dad's '39 Chevy coupe one morning. Coming up to the Gateway Junction just outside Ontario, he didn't slow down as we drove up to the flashing red light. We were going way too fast for a right-angle turn. I asked what he was doing. He replied, "Hell, I can make this corner at forty miles an hour." A '39 Chevy coupe cannot make a right-angle turn doing forty miles an hour. However, it can roll. The car needed a lot of bodywork, but neither of us was injured, thank God.

I was still working for Bob when Betty went into labor with our second child. Kathy was a beautiful baby, but something was wrong. She was jaundiced; her kidneys weren't functioning properly; and the doctor didn't believe she would survive. I was called into the waiting room and held my sweet little girl while my mother talked to the doctor. Mom called me to the phone. Bob Wolfe was on the line. He had no one to do my 2:00 a.m. milk run. I tried to explain what was happening, but he insisted that I needed to do the run, hinting that I might lose the job if I didn't show. I wanted to be with our baby and Betty, but I needed that job. I left the baby with my mother and went to work. Kathy died later that morning. That was over sixty years ago, but I still tear up when I think of that night. At the end of the shift I gave Bob my notice. I loved the job, but I would not work for someone who was so hard-hearted. Two weeks later, we loaded up the car and a small trailer and headed for The Dalles, Oregon.

Bob's son, Ted, later told me that the whole thing was my mom's doing. She was afraid I couldn't handle the situation and might get into a fight with the doctor, so she had phoned Bob. She told him to get me out of there...no matter what he had to do. It was the hardest thing I had faced up to at that time. I did break down, but I didn't "break-down." We later found that Betty was Rh negative and I was Rh positive, a problem little understood in the 1950s. It was not the last time we lost a child due to the Rh factor. We would lose Rosemary just a few years later.

Chapter Notes

[1]This is a transcription of the original letter, which was found in Gary's desk following his death in 2018. It is easy to overlook the fact that Gary was experiencing a reasonably happy functioning family when Wanda asked him to drop out of school and move back to Payette, Idaho.

[2]As an aside about "making do," a few years later Gary took old Highway 19 from The Dalles to Payette. His old Model A required a quart of oil every few miles. He stopped to visit Buzz Boemer's dad in Condon, Oregon. Mr. Boemer took the hood off and welded a five-gallon can to the two rods that secured the radiator. Then he fashioned a drip valve by drilling a small hole in the bottom of the can and inserting an adjustable screw. Gary filled the can with used motor oil, which dripped directly into the engine. With two extra five-gallon pails of oil in the trunk and the occasional stop at service stations along the way, he finished his trip.

[3]Smudge pots were orchard heaters consisting of a large round pot for oil with a small chimney coming out the center. Pots were set between the trees to produce a thick smog composed of smoke, carbon dioxide, and water vapor. Smudging generally went out of practice in the 1970s due to

high oil prices and environmental concerns.

[4]"Turd birds" were quite popular in the 1970s. A turd bird was handcrafted from a horse chip by spraying it with lacquer and adding feathers for the wings and tail. Tooth picks or small twigs were used for the legs. Tiny google eyes and a small plastic beak finished each creation. They were sold at Stuckey's service stations. Some tourists tried to collect one from each state. When and why Gary began using the term is not known.

Betty and Gary - 1949

DYNAMITE HEAD

EB'S CANCER HAD gone into remission, and he had moved Betty's mom and youngest sister, Patsy, to The Dalles. We arrived at the Allen's in a 1940 Plymouth sedan. It was in good shape for an older car, but the battery was shot. The car had to be pushed for rolling starts, and I couldn't afford to replace the battery. We were there a couple days when Eb asked me to go for a drive. We parked on a hill and walked several blocks to a used car lot. I thought he was looking for himself. Then he told me that I needed something reliable for going back and forth to work. I tried to tell him that I had a good car. I just needed a battery.

An enthusiastic young car salesman met us at the lot. Eb shook his hand, pointed at a Plymouth of the same year and make as mine, and insisted on taking it for a drive. The salesman tossed him the keys and away we went. I found the whole thing confusing. I didn't need a car; I couldn't afford a car; I certainly wouldn't buy what I already owned. Eb drove around several blocks and then parked in front of my Plymouth. He popped the hood on both cars and proceeded to swap the batteries. He told me to get in the dealer's vehicle while he pushed to get it started, and we drove back to the dealership. Eb returned the keys and chastised the salesman for sending us out with a bad battery. We then walked back to my car. My father-in-law had no conscience when helping the "haves" share with the "have-nots." He figured the car dealership could afford a new battery whereas I couldn't.

Eb soon had me working with him at Inland Navigation as a longshoreman. Barges came up the Columbia River to The Dalles where goods were transferred to rail cars and trucks for shipment to the interior. The work was hard, hot, and dangerous. Three men in the welding shop were killed during the six weeks I worked there. Temperatures in The Dalles regularly break 100 degrees, so we were issued boots with one and a half-inch soles to protect our feet from the hot metal decks.

I will never forget the day a stack of steel sheets had to be unloaded from a barge and stacked in the warehouse. Each sheet was four feet wide, eight feet high and a quarter inch thick. Total weight per sheet was over 300 pounds. We all groaned at the thought. Eb walked over to the pile, turned and said, "I'll bet my paycheck that I can stack these sheets by myself." Crew members thought he was crazy and so did I. Three men were willing to put their checks on the line. I might have too if he hadn't been my father-in-law. Eb only asked that we slide the steel sheets one at a time off the boat onto the dock. As each panel slid off the pile, Eb took hold of the sides and walked it on its corners into the warehouse. He then let it fall, allowing its large flat surface to glide into place with the natural support of the air. He knew what he was doing. When he finished, I asked, "You're not going to take their money, are you?" He did. He figured they would have taken his. Besides, they should have known that he wouldn't make a bet he couldn't win!

The first time I saw a man killed on a job was at Inland Navigation. A large truck had pulled in needing a tire repaired. The bigger tires were mounted on a split rim. A split rim had a locking ring that was held in place by the tire pressure. A ten by twenty-inch tire with 105 pounds of air pressure can exert up to 40,000 pounds of pressure against the rim flange. Before safety cages were introduced, mechanics normally reached through the back side of the rim to inflate the tire. Even then you could be badly injured if the locking ring blew loose. A young guy about my age was squatting with one knee on the tire as he inflated it. The locking ring hadn't been properly inserted. When it blew, the guy was thrown over six feet and lost the top half of his head. Holy cow! I was only nineteen years old and pretty shook up. There had to be a better way to make a living.

About that time, Dale and Nancy and their little boy, David, joined us. Dale said that loggers were needed in Eight Mile, a tiny little community not far from The Dalles. It was located "eight miles" up Willow Creek from the Columbia River. We could design and build our own cabins, have unlimited access to hunting and fishing, and make good wages. We were all teenagers or just barely over and it seemed like a great opportunity.

Betty and I decided to build a simple one-room cabin with a four-foot wall running through the middle separating the sleeping area from the living room. Dale, Nancy, Betty, and I had a great deal of fun working together. Terry and David had their little cowboy hats and toy pistols to keep them busy. There are always certain hazards that come with new territory. One afternoon, Dale happened by the scrap pile where the boys were playing and heard a timber rattler give its deadly warning. He smashed the snake's head with a plank just inches from Terry. Once the cabins were livable, Dale and I were off to the woods while Betty and Nancy put finishing touches on the cabins.

I soon found out why logging is rated as the most dangerous occupation in the country. I was working on a landing, that's the site where logs are stacked and cut to length in preparation for loading. Our landing had a large boom with a steel cable and hook for handling logs. The operator was swinging the boom around just as I was climbing the far side of the landing. I saw the steel hook the instant before it hit me in the forehead, knocking me off the landing and down an eighty-foot slide. The operator was sure he had killed me, but when they pulled me up the hill I began groaning and coughing. I went back to work about a week later but started having heart palpitations. The doctor told me the palpitations were fear related and in time would fade away.

Logging shuts down in the spring due to the winter break-up. Eb had picked up a job hauling poles to the mine in Stibnite, Idaho and took me along. The antimony found in Stibnite was so important for the production of bullets during the war that men could work there in lieu of serving in the military. By the time we arrived, the operation was slowing down, but I started a job cleaning the huge industrial furnaces. The job consisted of smearing mud on the butts of long poles and then sledgehammering them into the exhaust ports of the furnaces. I stayed less than a month. No amount of money is worth what those miners suffered. Within weeks men's eyelids began turning inside out from the toxic chemicals. That was not for me.

When I returned to The Dalles, the Eastern Oregon Tuberculosis Hospital needed employees. Few today realize that tuberculosis, "the white plague," killed far more people than the Bubonic plague of the Middle Ages. The only treatment seemed to be fresh air, sunshine, and good nutrition. Months, sometimes years, of bed rest were required while the body cured itself[1]. The Dalles, because of the hot dry climate, was considered an ideal location. I worked in the laundry. Believe it or not, employees working in the sanatorium were less likely to contract the disease than those working in regular hospitals. Why? We knew what we were working with. Nonetheless, routine check-ups were required every three months.

Incredibly, some doctors recommended the smoking of menthol cigarettes as a way of soothing the lungs. I soon learned better. Part of my job was disposing of diseased lungs that had been surgically removed. The lungs of heavy smokers were black with cigarette tar and oozed dark liquid mucus. Betty and I had always shared a cigarette and coffee in the mornings, but what I saw at the san convinced me to quit. Betty wouldn't hear of it. She had been smoking since she was about thirteen and had no intention of quitting. She could be so hardheaded. I'm sure she blew smoke in my direction just to torment me.

While working at the san, I picked up part-time work with the Oregon State Police. The state was cracking down on prostitution. I was paid to circulate among the various bars, get to know which ones had pleasure rooms, and then call in the occasional raid to catch girls with their johns. What other job will pay you to go barhopping every night and pay for the booze? Problem was, I commiserated with the bar owners and the young women. I remembered Louis Anchustegui helping my own mother and feeding me sandwiches out the back door of his bar. Little Wanda, who ran a brothel in Ontario, had seemed like a pretty nice lady to me. I also understood that the "pleasure" was often one-sided. Many young women were doing what they felt necessary to feed themselves and their children. The raids made their lives worse, not better.

I was sent to stake out the Ace of Hearts[2] bar in Hood River. I spent several nights there, enough to get to know the bartender and a few of the women that worked upstairs. They were pretty nice, and it wasn't easy staying downstairs. I kept reminding myself that I was a married man and my expense account only covered drinks. These women were not coerced into the business like so many caught in the "white slave trade" of the big cities. Bill and Marta, the owners of the bar, treated the girls with respect and were quick to help them if there was trouble. The night of my first raid I sat at the bar and asked to see Bill. I told him that I couldn't answer any questions, but it was important that all the women be somewhere else at 2:00 a.m. When closing time came, I called in the raid. A half-hour later, policemen stormed the building to find no one there. I was called into headquarters. I assured the chief that the girls and their johns were there when I called, that the Vice Squad had simply been too slow in responding. After two more weeks of "undercover" work with no success, my services were no longer required. The Police Chief said I was too softhearted for undercover work. About a month later I received a plain envelope in the mail. It contained a thousand dollars and a simple thank you from, "Bill, Marta, and the girls."

That spring, construction was ramping up for The Dalles Dam[3]. Drillers and blasters were paid far more than laundry workers or tree fallers. I would never admit that I couldn't do a job. I mean, how much experience does it take to run a jackhammer? Or to plug a hole with dynamite? Fortunately, my boss recognized my lack of experience within the first half hour on the job and coached me on the basics. I thought he was just being nice, but he was looking after himself and the crew. Goodbye "palpitations" and hello "dynamite head." If logging is rated as the most dangerous job, working with explosives is a close second. Stories of men blowing themselves up through carelessness or losing arms and legs through poor judgment abounded. A faulty fuse meant loss of a day, because you never check a delayed charge short of twelve hours. Blasting myths insured that we were careful...no shortcuts! I soon developed debilitating headaches and nausea from contact with nitroglycerin. My head throbbed so bad, I was afraid to bat an eye. With time, blasters acquire a temporary immunity, but a couple days off work and it's back to square one. Blasters earned good money. In just a few months I paid off our Spartanette trailer. I figured the pain was worth the gain.

Eb picked up night work servicing and parking the haul trucks used on the dam. He soon hatched a scheme to make extra money. The entire Indian settlement of Celilo, an area where, according to the archeologists, Indians had lived for over 10,000 years, would soon be covered with water. Eb figured that tourists would pay a fortune for Indian artifacts. The easiest way to procure such treasures was to make your own, so he began collecting old pottery. Once filled with dirt and rubble from the dam site, the "artifacts" were stashed in the beds of various trucks. When the trucks dumped debris the following day, the artifacts were discovered by...you know who. Eb wasn't the only person digging for artifacts, and when the "ancient" pots and bowls were discovered, construction very nearly came to a stop. The authorities never uncovered how the pottery came to be on the site but for Eb, the project was a bust.

When we lost a man because of a delayed fuse, I decided to return to logging at Eight Mile. Two weeks later, an empty logging truck pulled up to the back side of our landing. We waited for the driver to come around...and waited...and waited...and finally went to see what he was doing. We found him beneath a large log that had rolled off the pile as he got out of his truck. I'm generally not superstitious, but it seemed someone was getting killed at every turn, not to mention the "normal" deaths I had seen at the sanatorium. We moved back to Idaho. A month later, I got word that Bill, my foreman at the dam, had been killed in a blasting accident.

Chapter Notes

[1]With the discovery of streptomycin in 1943, sanatoriums began to close. By the mid-1950's tuberculosis was no longer considered a major public health risk.

[2]Fictitious name.

[3]A congressional hearing cleared the way for construction of The Dalles Dam by concluding that the destruction of Celilo Falls did not violate the Treaty of 1855. The treaty guaranteed indigenous fishing rights and access to traditional fishing stations to the Cayuse, Umatilla, and Walla Walla First Nations. When the dam was completed in 1957, evidence of a native settlement at Celilo and a fishing trade that spanned nearly 10,000 years disappeared within hours. Tradition maintains that a sealed jar containing the original treaty was imbedded in an oak tree near Mill Creek just outside The Dalles. Since an oak can live up to 1,000 years, the tree was meant to symbolize a perpetual agreement. The tree was still standing on the property of Treaty Oak Orchards in the 1960s.

THE LITTLE RED HOUSE

THE TIMING COULDN'T have been better. The Marshall Company, which specialized in hardwood church furniture, was hiring for their woodworking shop. At the same time, an elderly lady named Abercrombie wanted to move closer to her children. She lived in a little red shake house on 7th Avenue North in Payette. It was a story and a half house with a living room, kitchen, and bedroom downstairs. The upstairs was divided into two large bedrooms. Mrs. Abercrombie was thrilled to trade the house straight across for our Spartanette trailer. Overnight, I had a good job and we owned our own home. Not bad for a husband and wife ages twenty and seventeen.

My idea of marriage was that men bring home the check and women keep the house and children. Betty was only seventeen and wasn't one to stay home or keep house if she didn't have to. Why make the bed if you're going to use it again? Why wash dishes until you need them? Her cooking was basically anything that could be fried or boiled. We ate a lot of beans and goulash. That quickly changed when Jean Christiansen, our next-door neighbor, invited Betty over for coffee. Jean was in her early twenties and was an immaculate housekeeper. Beds made; dishes washed; floors polished; cabinets organized; even a plan for meals. As Betty was leaving, Jean said, "Thanks so much for coming over. Tomorrow we can have coffee at your place." When I came home that night, I found Betty in the kitchen scrubbing the floor. Our bed had been made; the dishes were washed; and supper was on the table. Jean would never know how much her friendship changed our household.

Betty soon transformed our house into a real home. One thing I admired about her, she was one of the most hospitable people I've ever known. The door was always open; the coffee pot was always on; and there was always an extra place at the table. If the soup needed an extra cup of water, she made it happen. When the Allens moved from Texas, they brought along good old southern hospitality. While Betty worked on the inside, I set to work on the yard. A small pasture was behind our house, so we had a fenced backyard with a detached garage and shed. Money was still tight, but at the Marshall Company I used my breaks to build outdoor furniture, including a swing and rocking horse for Terry.

Someone gave us a greyhound named Shorty. Shorty was a wanderer, but always came home. Unfortunately for the neighbors, but to Terry's delight, he regularly brought things from other people's backyards: baseball gloves, shoes (usually just one of a pair), doormats, clothing, and anything else Shorty could get in his mouth. We didn't have him long. A friend dropped in one night and said that a pack of dogs had run in front of his car and he had hit something "as big as a cow." He had stopped and checked to see what it was, but there was nothing along the Street. Terry and Bill, my little brother, found a deceased Shorty next to the house the next day.

Betty and I were so young and everything we did was an adventure. When Christmas came around in 1953, we went all out in making it special for Terry. He was just a month and a half short of turning three years old. I had six puppies in the garage. I finally chose a little black spaniel with a white patch on her chest and we returned the rest. The puppy reminded me of a miniature version of Andy. We went for a drive that evening so a neighbor could slip the dog into the house. When we came home, a little black ball of fur ran through the kitchen. How exciting! We named her Dinah. She became a great companion for Terry, and later for Vicki and Liz. "Someone's in the Kitchen with Dinah" was Terry's favorite song.

We arranged for a couple visits from Santa that year. One night while sitting in the living room having some story time, Betty assured Terry that Santa was always watching to see who was "naughty and nice." Bad boys would find lumps of coal and washcloths in their stockings on Christmas day. Good boys would find candy and toys. Terry looked around and saw a bearded old man peering through the living room window. Some kids would be terrified, but not him. He ran and opened the front door and called out, "Santa! Come back!" as a friend of mine from work went scurrying through the shrubs. "Santa" came back on Christmas Eve. Terry answered a knock at the front door and old George stood there in his olive-green work coat and black stocking cap with a gunnysack over his shoulder. As he began to pull out the toys, Terry asked, "Santa, where's your red coat?" George answered, "My red coat is for special occasions. These are my work clothes." George ate a couple cookies, drank a glass of milk, and left with a "Ho! Ho! Ho!" before Terry could ask about his reindeer or why he hadn't come down the chimney. Looking back, Betty and I were just a couple of kids enjoying our own kids as they came along.

One day Betty saw an ad on television that she had to show me. A company selling plastic wrap showed a demonstration where the actor covered a pitcher of milk with the wrap and then held it upside down. The wrap sealed and held tight, keeping the milk in the pitcher. Betty practiced with a pitcher and water with successful results. When I came home from work, she filled the pitcher with milk, covered it with plastic wrap, and turned it upside down. We both got a big surprise. I'll let you guess....

We had our spats, the biggest one being Betty's desire for more independence. She wanted to have a job and make her own money. I believed a woman's place was at home. Besides, she was pregnant about half the time. My mom's influence didn't help. One morning, Betty and I were having a heated discussion about something I wanted done while I was at work. Mom happened to drop in for coffee as I was about to slam the door and head off. I paused outside the front door and heard my mother saying, "Look Betty, don't argue with him. Just agree with what he says and once he leaves, do what you want." Several years later when Betty could legally drink, Mom would occasionally take her for an afternoon cocktail. Those afternoon cocktails contributed to what became a life-long habit. I blame Mom for some of the problems we faced.

Norm Potter, a friend from my teenage years, introduced me to the National Guard. Finally, I would get a taste of the military, but without the risk of being under live fire. The Guard was great fun, kind of like being in the Boy Scouts, only on a higher level. Every weekend there were drills and training. I learned to march. I learned the army way to shoot. I learned to throw grenades. I learned to drive jeeps. Most importantly, I learned about tanks. We were attached to the 116th Cavalry Brigade out of Boise. The tank is the modern version of the horse, only a lot more predictable...most of the time. When driving a World War II tank, the driver can't see where the tank is going. A spotter sits above him and uses foot pressure on his shoulders to give directions. The tank maneuvers like a skid steer loader:

one track holds while the other keeps rolling. When equipped with the huge metal tracks, it literally "tears" up the road when making a turn. I quickly learned that you best respond to that shoulder pressure. I remember sitting as a spotter for Norm as we moved a tank through the Gateway Junction between Payette and Ontario. I had given foot pressure for a short turn. The steering locked and we drove right through the Gateway Junction Dance Hall. That was an expensive maneuver. I was grateful that Norm, who was my superior, was doing the driving.

Our unit went to Fort Lewis, Washington for extra training. I soon found that soldiering can be the most boring job on earth when there isn't a war. Officers are adept at creating jobs. You've heard of digging a hole and then refilling. We learned the same principle cleaning tanks. So long as we looked busy, Captain Gael, our company commander, was happy and wouldn't assign us to yet another "keep busy" project. We soon figured out when Captain Gael would be preoccupied elsewhere and managed to "borrow" a jeep. Bill Cochrane, my buddy Forest's brother, lived in the army compound. He took us for some good runs around the base and local area.

Our unit entered a couple war games during my stint. It was a blast...in every way! Where else can you go into battle with virtually unlimited ammunition and avoid killing anyone or worse, getting killed yourself. Theoretically, I was killed a couple times. The bombs used in the games discharged huge clouds of a flour-like powder. Once covered with flour, you reported to a muster station and were considered a casualty. It was game over for you. A buddy of mine and I were both "killed" in a bomb blast and managed to come back to life by jumping into a local river and rinsing off the evidence. I died a couple times and lived to fight again. In some ways, that has been the story of my life.

After two years of giving up weekends and holidays for Guard duty, I had had enough. My first Sunday morning at home as a free man was being celebrated with a family breakfast. Then came a knock at the door. Two Military Policemen stood on the steps ready to escort me to Guard duty. I tried to explain, but they took me by the arms, led me to their jeep, and drove me to the Armory. Norm grinned as they led me into his office, "Welcome back, soldier!" I hadn't seen him since the previous weekend when I had finished my term of service. I remembered barhopping and tying on a real bender. What I didn't remember was driving back to the Armory and signing up for another two years. The second two years were not as fun as the first. As for Norm, he stayed in the Guard for twenty years and then retired with a partial military pension.

Norm and I remained life-long friends. We had our differences. I can't say that I'm religious in the sense of church attendance, but I have a strong belief in God. I've had too many close calls not to. Norm saw Christianity as one big fairy tale created for people who needed a crutch to get through life. We had some heated discussions, but he claimed to be a staunch atheist. I got my point across when the two of us fought a fire together at Zigzag Mountain near Mount Hood in Oregon. With a shift in the wind we found ourselves running for our lives. Resting on a rock pile, surrounded by dirt and ash, I asked Norm, "Who were you praying to?" He shot back, "Go to hell Roth." Anyone who prays in a pinch and believes in hell, must believe in something.

I don't know if Betty ever totally recovered from the loss of Kathy. She battled depression throughout most of our marriage. A lot of guilt accompanies the death of a child, especially when there is no logical explanation. Her family's stories of ghosts and death angels may have haunted her. I was too immature to provide the emotional support she needed. There was also a near tragedy involving Terry that deeply affected her. She was driving home from the grocery store in our 1946 Dodge. The back doors on those cars were called "suicide doors," because they were hinged at the rear of the car. If a suicide door swung open while the car was moving, the wind would catch it, forcing it wide open. The doors were dangerous for pedestrians and passengers. Terry was sitting in the back seat playing with the doorknob as Betty was driving home from the grocery store. He accidentally pulled the door handle and was jerked from the car as the wind caught the door. Betty looked in the rearview mirror to see her little boy sprawled unconscious in the street. The left rear wheel had creased the right side of his head leaving tread marks and the indentation of his ear. He was one sick little boy. It was a long time before she would let him out of her sight.

We started attending the First Christian Church. They had a good Sunday School for Terry and offered the moral and spiritual support we needed. Betty was more serious than me, but we became quite active. Hard to believe, but the two of us sang duets for some services. About this time, the summer of 1953, we purchased our first television. I recall climbing to the roof to install and position the antenna for reception of two stations, Channel 2 and Channel 7. Betty's two favorite programs were Liberace, a flamboyant pianist, and Oral Roberts, a charismatic televangelist. Roberts preached faith healing and the abundant life through Jesus. With what we were going through, I'm not certain how encouraging he was. We weren't experiencing a lot of healing, and life was a struggle.

Betty's depression increased. Sometimes she took to bed for several days at a time. I don't know what I would have done without Mom's help with Terry and Vicki. Things came to a crisis when Betty experienced what she described as a bright light in the form of a dove coming through the bedroom window. She claimed that it filled the room with light and hovered around her. Our pastor believed it was the presence of an evil spirit and refused to come into the house. We made the decision to move. Rumor had it that the older lady who bought the house ended up in a psychiatric ward. It was said that she went into deep trances, spending hour after hour writing manuscripts in some unknown language.

Shortly before our move, Eb asked his daughters to come to The Dalles for a family visit. He was still dealing with a slow-growing cancer and had just suffered a minor heart attack. Nancy, Betty, and Patsy were together with their folks for a week. Eb took them to dinner, hosted family picnics, and visited late into the nights. After a lifetime of alcoholism, he had quit drinking and was determined to make things right with his family.

The daughters were shocked to find he had even reconciled with his brother Will. The brothers hadn't talked to each other in over twenty years, and Will's name was never mentioned in Eb's presence. Betty said that the rift had started with a woman. As young men, Eb and his brother had a falling out over a call girl. While the woman waited in the back of their truck, the brothers argued over who would be first. Neither one wanted "seconds." As the altercation heated up, Will grabbed Eb's hat, threw it on the ground, and proceeded to jump on it. No one knows how the argument ended, but I can vouch for the fact that the Allens were slow to let go of insults. Betty hadn't fallen far from the tree on that count. She might forgive a slight, but she rarely forgot. Once when confronted with Jesus's teaching about extending forgiveness, she responded, "It says, 'if he repents!'"

The visit was better than any medication the doctor could have ordered. Betty came home ready for our next move to a little green house on the edge of town.

GARY AND BETTY HAD A FARM

NEW YEAR'S EVE, 1957, I met a fellow at a bar who was intent on selling a twenty-acre farm. It was located five miles out of town and included a chicken house, shop, and small barn. It came, livestock and equipment included. I could buy it for $1,500 if I would make the deal that night. The following morning, I let Betty know that I had put $750 down on a farm. *Lesson to self: never make a major decision without looking at what you're buying and always consult your wife first.* We drove out to see the place. The house was a wreck. The ceiling was sagging. The paint was worn through on the old board floors. Cardboard paneling was bulging in various places along the walls. There was an old oil stove in the front room and a woodstove in the kitchen. The house needed wiring. There was no plumbing. The outhouse was filthy, had an awful stench, and was home to swarms of flies. A 1936 Ford pickup, a Case tractor that needed repairs, and an old Farmall tractor were parked beside the shop.

Betty was appalled. It would snow in hell before she would live in that house. I convinced her that we could remodel the house before making the move. In the meantime, the livestock, which seemed like such a good thing the night before, required a trip every day for feeding. That meant working all day and spending an extra hour every night looking after a dozen rabbits, two goats, and three geese. Betty offered to look after the animals if she could use the car.

The very next day, she dropped me off at work with my admonition, "Make sure you don't get out of the ruts on the lane." That evening Betty didn't show up to drive me home. I bummed a ride after work. Betty was home, but the car was not in the driveway. She had left it about two yards off the lane at the farm with all four wheels sunk in mud and snow. She had figured that with the lane so rough and slippery, it only made sense to drive along the side. The snow cover gave the impression of a smooth, solid ride...NOT!

The animals weren't worth making a trip every night, so I asked our closest neighbor, Pio Fenicottero, if he would take them. On my next trip to the farm, the animals were gone. Pio had butchered the goats, geese, and rabbits. If I had known he wasn't going to raise them, I would have butchered them myself.

Come spring we made the move. There was so much to be done, building a new house might have been easier. We brought in a combination electric-woodstove for the kitchen, but I needed to reroute the old knob and tube wiring in the attic. Knob and tube hadn't been used for construction for over twenty years, so you can imagine some of the issues. I told Betty, "Whatever you do, don't turn on the stove while I'm working on wiring in the attic."

Well, she couldn't resist. I was just cutting into a wire when a surge of electricity ran down one arm, through my body, and out the sole of my right shoe. I screamed what sounded like a death cry and dropped through the ceiling.

Betty was already out the front door and halfway to the neighbors, afraid of what I might do. *Another lesson to self: always turn off the breaker or remove the fuse before working on electrical.*

An old-fashioned hand pump in the kitchen supplied water for the house. Outside, a massive hand pump provided water for the livestock and garden. The handle, an eight-foot piece of angle iron, lifted above shoulder height on the upswing and required both hands and full body weight to get started. Within the first month the handle caught Betty on the side of the head. She had turned to shout at one of the kids and let go. The flywheel kept the handle moving, which knocked Betty out on the downswing. To keep the peace, I installed an electric pump the following week. We still didn't have plumbing or an indoor bathroom, but it was a start.

Betty worried that we would never see any of our friends once we moved from town. The opposite was true. It was a short drive and we had a large yard, perfect for barbecues and kid's games. Hardly a summer weekend went by that one couple or another didn't come to visit. My buddies were more than willing to help with renovations. I recall a Saturday with Buzz and Norm and a couple cases of beer when we drywalled the back porch. We thought we were real professionals. The following day, when I was sober, I looked at our work and realized I would have to tear it all out and start over again. The second time, I didn't ask for help.

We bathed only once a week. Water was heated on the kitchen stove and poured into a large galvanized tub. The whole family used the same water, beginning with the kids and ending with me. One summer weekend while Betty and the kids were visiting friends, I decided to enjoy a good soak outside. I poured fresh steaming hot water into the tub, laid my clothes on the grass, and settled in with my arms and legs hanging over the sides. A small Piper Cub flew over, circled around, and started diving over the yard as I grabbed my clothes and scrambled into the house. A few minutes later, a car came ripping along a back road and turned down our lane. Joe Babcock, a friend from town, had landed his plane at a small airport about a half-mile behind our house. He wanted me to know that he was keeping an eye on me.

Those were some of our best years. We regularly played pinochle with various friends. We would take the whole family and put the children to sleep on the sofas and floor while we played till the early morning. One time, I decided it was time to head home after I had played the same card three times. Everyone was so bleary-eyed that nobody noticed.

We took up water skiing on the Snake River. I had learned to get up from a sitting start off the dock. Can you believe it? A nail caught my suit and exposed my beautiful behind. I motioned to the boat to keep going! We also tried what we called a "surfboard." A handle was attached directly to the board by two ropes. The board was attached by a single rope to the boat. The skier stood on the board and maneuvered with his feet. You could almost fly on that board. Joe Babcock gave his boat full throttle to see just how good I was. I came off the board on a turn and hit the water so hard I got a severe concussion.

I must have been out of my mind, because while convalescing I decided to hand dig the hole for a septic tank. The top six inches of soil in southern Idaho is fantastic, but from there on it's hardpan clay. A pick, shovel, and a lot of muscle were required to dig that hole. It was not good work for a man recovering from a head injury.

On the farm being laid up doesn't mean there's no work to do; horses have to be watered; chickens have to be fed; cows have to be milked. We had a young Jersey cow we called Bossy. She was a playful little thing. One time she tossed her head at me as she came through the barn door, caught me under the ribs with a horn, and pushed me against the wall. Fun and games for her, but not for me. While still recovering from the concussion, I went to the barn one morning with a splitting headache. That morning Bossy wanted to play. Every time she came to the barn door, she dodged to the left and ran around the corner. Then she peeked out to see if I was coming after her. I was in no mood for games. By the third time she pulled that stunt, I was hiding beside the corner of the barn with a two-by-four. When she stuck her head around the corner, I clobbered her so hard that I knocked a horn off. Blood was everywhere. Poor thing nearly died by the time the vet arrived. I sold her the following week. Any man that will do that to an animal shouldn't have one. It was a while before we had another cow. I still feel bad about it.

Elizabeth was born while we lived on the farm. She was our fifth baby in eight years. She was such a little cutie and never a problem. She reminded me of my younger sister, Sally. Dr. Kotas expressed concern for Betty. She was young and in fairly good health, but the pregnancies had taken their toll. Kathy and Rosemarie had both died shortly after birth. There was no guarantee that another baby would fare any better. Betty lived in fear of another pregnancy, so I scheduled a vasectomy.

We men are sensitive to what goes on down there. Dr. Kotas assured me that it would not affect my manhood. In fact, it should make life a lot more enjoyable. He arranged to meet me at the hospital in Ontario. On the given day I was nervous as hell. I showed up at St. Alphonsus Hospital and took a seat in the main lobby. When Dr. Kotas didn't show, I began pacing back and forth. An older nun, Sister Agnes, approached and asked why I was there. I told her I was waiting for Dr. Kotas. Sister checked at the admittance desk and informed me that Dr. Kotas wasn't scheduled at St.

Alphonsus that day. Again, she asked "why" I was there. I glanced at my belt buckle and whispered, "vasectomy." Sister Agnes glared at me and muttered, "I think you're at the wrong hospital!"

The kids were always full of surprises. One summer evening I was walking out to do chores and noticed that the shop windows were pockmarked with BB holes. Inside, mound after mound of shattered jars mixed with various screws and bolts littered the shelves above the workbench. Those jars represented hours of sorting through the sweepings at the Marshall Company during my years on the shop floor. I rarely raised a hand on any of my kids. Discipline was left to Betty, but this time I headed for the house. Terry can be thankful that his Grandma Wanda had picked him up that afternoon for a one-week trip to the Payette Lakes near McCall, Idaho. His Uncle Bill, who was from Mom's second marriage, and only two years older than Terry, had been his accomplice. Until the end of time, Terry's treasured BB gun will rest at the bottom of the old privy.

Vicki created her own challenges. She was such a little turd bird! Everything she tried, no matter how innocent, turned into a disaster. Terry and one of his friends decided to start ant farms. They dug up a colony of tiny black ants and placed them in a quart jar. Vicki had to have an ant farm too. The problem, she dug up a hill of red ants. If it hadn't already been coined, the phrase "ants in your pants" could have come from her. She must have been attacked by the whole colony – in her hair, up and down both legs, in her pants and panties.

After we put in the bathroom, I one day glanced in to see Vicki facing the toilet with her panties down and pee running all over the floor. She was determined to pee the same way "daddy" did. Then, not wanting a bath, she managed to escape buck naked and head down the lane to the neighbors.

When a salesman came to discuss new siding for the house, Vicki tagged along as he prepared his estimate. She kept saying, "Mister...mister...do you know what we kids are?" We were talking business and trying to ignore her, but she wouldn't give up. "Mister, do you know what we kids are?" I finally looked at her and said, "Okay, Vic, just what are you kids?" She smiled, batted her eyes, and said, "Just a bunch of dirty little shit-ass kids!" She didn't get that language from me.

Betty had occasional bouts of severe depression going back to when we lost Kathy. Terry's accident and then the death of Rosemary had compounded her struggle. A late-night phone call in 1960 took her to the depths. "Betty, it's bad news, your dad's had a massive heart attack and...." Betty burst into the most pitiful wail I've ever heard. She wouldn't be consoled, but kept sobbing, "No...no...no!" She had always felt a special connection to Eb. Though a daughter, she felt she was his "boy." He had taught her to shoot, to drive, to hunt: to do all the things boys do with their dads. He was a heavy smoker and so was she. He was a heavy drinker, and she followed in his footsteps. With his death, she felt disconnected emotionally and didn't recover for a long time.

My mom took the kids while Betty and I drove to The Dalles to help with the funeral. It was a strange experience. Eb had anticipated his death. When Faye approached the funeral home, the undertaker showed us a casket he claimed Eb had chosen the week before. I was upset that he would stoop so low in trying to make a sale. Before I could speak, he said, "Mr. Allen insisted he wanted a casket with an inner spring mattress." Eb had always said that he wanted an inner spring mattress for his final rest. We went to the local department store for a suit. The merchant had a fitted suit ready for pick-up that Eb had purchased the week before. Eb had made his own arrangements at the funeral home. Everything was pre-paid. Later, Faye found that he had also cleared all their debts.

A graveside service was arranged on a miserably cold, cloudy day. I went to a local shop to purchase a camera. The only thing available was an old Kodak Brownie. I didn't feel very assured of getting any quality photos. The weather was getting more and more overcast. There were occasional showers of rain. The casket was open, so family members could say a final goodbye. As Betty paused and placed her hand on the lip of the coffin, two large tears ran down Eb's cheeks. Betty collapsed. The commotion that followed delayed the service for two hours. The camera produced only one clear photo, a picture of Eb in his casket. In the photograph he is surrounded with an aura of light.

Betty always had an interest in the occult but after her dad's death, she delved even deeper. Ouija boards and astrology fascinated her. Betty and her sister, Patsy, learned to raise tables. They could place their hands on a three-legged table and ask a question. The table would tilt and tap out the answer with one leg; one tap for yes, two taps for no. If they asked for a person's age, the table would tap out the answer. It was spooky. We went through a stage where the Ouija was consulted before and after almost everything we did. I was getting disgusted with it. It seems Betty felt a need to connect with the "other".

Betty became involved with a medium named Nola. Nola was convinced that Betty had a psychic gift. She told Betty that if she set a plain glass of water by her bed at night, the following morning she could look into the glass and see the events of her day. Betty never tried it. She was afraid of going too far into something that had an aura of evil. The Ouija board and astrological tables were set aside.

Just before moving to the farm, I had gone to work with Wells and Davies, a local slaughterhouse. Now I was feeding livestock at 5:00 a.m., starting my job at 6:00, and coming home for a short nap at 2:30 p.m. Then I crawled on the tractor for several hours of field work before collapsing in bed. On weekends, I occasionally dug graves: six foot-eight inches deep, thirty inches wide, and seven feet long for ten dollars a grave. I also painted flagpoles, fifteen dollars a pole. Looking back, I realize that I was good at making money, but not so good at spending time with the family. We made the most of our weekends, but that was not enough.

The farm was great for me and the kids, but there was a downside for Betty. During the week I went to work every day and was around other people. When I came home, I was on the tractor or doing chores. Terry and Vicki were at school all day. Betty was only twenty-one or twenty-two years old, pregnant, and home alone all week when we moved there. Before long she was stuck at home with a growing baby. I must give her credit, she was energetic. We had a large garden, which she irrigated by hand. She filled our cellar, a dirt-walled pit underneath the back porch, with home-canned fruit and vegetables. We purchased old laying hens for about twenty-five cents each. They continued to lay the occasional egg before Betty took them to the chopping block. I bought a cow and we raised a calf.

I remember purchasing a 1957 Dodge Coronet. It was a beauty. I came home about six-thirty one night and found Betty waiting to use the car. She was planning a girls' night out with Beverly Boemer. I refused to give her the keys. The next thing I knew, our old Farmall tractor was headed down the lane. Beverly brought her home early the next morning. I found the Farmall parked in an alley behind the V-Club, the most popular bar in Payette. In the battle of the sexes, I didn't have a chance.

It must have been so hard for Betty. She took up hand braiding rugs with scrap upholstery. She briefly tried playing a steel lap guitar. She studied and took the exams for her GED. She stripped and refinished furniture. We purchased our first stereo and she soon had every album Elvis ever made. I wanted her to be a farm wife, but she wanted more. She was growing into a mature woman and struggling to find her own identity. There was a short time where she dyed or bleached her hair a different color every couple weeks. That stopped when she began to get boils on her scalp. She briefly took up oil painting and pastels. She wanted to work outside the home, but I didn't want a working wife, and someone had to be there for the kids. As far as I was concerned, we didn't need another breadwinner in the family.

Sometime after Eb's death we had a quarrel over Betty's smoking, and I refused to pick up cigarettes. Well, she had acquired all her dad's pipes and tobacco. The next time I came home I found Betty at the kitchen table puffing on a pipe. When the pipe tobacco ran out, she hitched Rock, an old workhorse we had for the kids, to a cart and drove to town. That week's cream money paid for a carton of Kools.

To stretch our dollars, I brought home the last vertebrae from the butchered hogs at Wells and Davies. The vertebrae reminded me of chicken necks and had long thin strings of good meat attached. Betty fried them and the kids loved them. Too bad my boss realized there might be commercial value in what we called "pig's tails." He put a stop to that. We regularly checked the local Simplot cellars for reject potatoes. Idaho potatoes are known across the country and it wasn't that difficult to cut off a bad spot or bruise and enjoy nature's finest. When Simplot needed to dump a load of rejected onions, I volunteered one of my fields. We salvaged what we could and invited all the neighbors to help themselves. What was left I spread on the field and plowed in as fertilizer. Betty and I had both grown up in poor families and knew how to make the most of every opportunity. In many ways we were a great team.

Betty and Gary with Terry, Elizabeth, and Vicki – Easter 1960

THE STORIES OF MY FATHER

AND ON THAT FARM...

OLD MCDONALD HAD had nothing on us when it came to farm animals. Let me introduce you to the barnyard family.

Dinah loved the farm. She had quite a nose and roamed the fields all day. She would have made a great pheasant dog if our neighbor, Henry Sailor, hadn't shot her through one front leg. Henry figured that anything crossing the fence between our properties was trespassing. A full front leg cast didn't stop that little dog from checking out the property every day, but the sound of a gun, or the sight of a stick with the rough shape of a gun, would send her under the house. Dinah was the sweetest little dog. We allowed her a couple litters of pups before having her spayed. Afterward, she onetime robbed a litter of kittens, carefully carrying two of the little things to her own bed where she tried to nurse them.

The only problem we ever had with Dinah had to do with our chickens. The Fenicottero's large male spaniel, Dusty, had wandered into our yard. Dusty and Dinah managed to get into the chicken coop. There was barking and squawking, blood and feathers, and the twang of bodies hitting the chicken wire. Fourteen hens were dead before I could get there. Dusty dodged under the fence and hightailed it for home. There was no escape for Dinah. I picked up a board and beat her while rubbing her nose in one dead bird after another. Terry and Vicki were outside the fence crying and pleading for me to stop. Then I chained Dinah to a tree with a dead chicken tied around her neck for the next week. It was either cure her or kill her. Pio and I had a brief falling out over our dogs. He shot Dusty and felt I should shoot Dinah.

Dinah tried so hard to get away from the chicken tied to her neck. She would turn her nose as far from it as possible. Vicki, who always had a special connection to dogs and cats, wanted to make things better for the poor little pooch. Somehow, she caught a live hen and tried to feed it to the dog. Dinah would have nothing of it. She was cured!

A neighbor gave the kids a little black puppy with the assurance that it wouldn't get very big. Not big, my foot. It was a Labrador Retriever. We named her Lady. Lady and Dinah had an interesting relationship. If we gave Dinah a piece of stale toast, she would soon dig a hole in the garden, deposit the toast, and carefully smooth loose dirt over it with her nose. A few minutes later Lady would appear, dig up the toast, and eat it.

No farm is complete without a cat. Ours was a big yellow tomcat named Tom. *How original!* He loved Vicki, but regularly flexed his claws when she got on his nerves. That was his warning. If not heeded, a painful scratch soon followed. I've seen that cat stalk and bring down a full-grown pheasant. Much to Tom's delight, the Sailors had six or eight pussycats. It wasn't long before Tom was hobbling around the farm with a cast on both front legs. I guess Henry wasn't that good of a shot.

There are lots of snakes in southern Idaho. When I plowed in the spring, the black snakes would follow along the furrows eating worms and other ground insects. Snakes outgrow their skins several times a year. Paper-like shed skins could be found throughout our property. One skin the kids brought home stretched across the full width of the car dash. Bull snakes, though not poisonous, had similar markings to rattlesnakes and were more aggressive than the black snakes. We found the occasional bull snake in the chicken coop. A large snake can swallow a whole egg. I usually killed any snakes we found in the yard. They had to be buried quite deep or Lady would dig them up. She would shake them as though she were breaking their necks and then drag them around the yard for a few days.

Lee brought us a big yellow dog that he had picked up at a truck stop in eastern Oregon. The dog resembled a large short-haired Labrador retriever in size, but not in disposition. We named him "Old Yeller". *Again, how original.* Not knowing if he could be trusted, I had him on a chain for the first while. Vicki claimed him as her own and made an immediate attachment. One day I was teasing Vicki and gave a playful tug on her pigtail. Yeller lunged and planted his teeth in my arm. He was strong and mean. He once took a run and broke his chain to chase after a couple horses up the hill from our farm. He was also a cat killer and in just a few minutes off his chain had quickly killed two of our younger cats. Old Yeller had to go.

I bought Tony, a little saddle horse for Terry. Tony wasn't mean, but he was ornery. He would carry Terry or Vicki about thirty or forty feet from the barn and then start crow hopping[1]. The kids would get scared and let him run back to the barn. I could yell at him from the yard and he would behave so long as I was in sight. If a kid fell off, I could count on spending the rest of the day trying to catch him.

Once I realized that Tony was too much horse for the kids, I traded him for a retired Clydesdale named Rock. Rock had been tangled up in an electric fence which left him with a bad heart. He could no longer do heavy labor, but he was perfect for our little farm. The Budweiser horses had nothing over Rock. He was a chestnut with blaze face, dark mane and tail, and white fetlocks. Rock weighed 2,000 pounds. He was big and strong and had been used to train younger horses. When hitched with another horse, Rock would tolerate no nonsense. If a workmate acted up or didn't pull, he would reach over with his teeth, take a mouthful of neck, and give it a painful shake. Otherwise he was quite gentle. It was not unusual to find Vicki in the pasture with both arms wrapped around one of Rock's rear legs giving the old guy a big hug. He would just swish his tail and keep grazing. I built a small stall on the outside wall of the barn. The kids could lead Rock into the stall and then climb a ladder to get on. Sometimes as many as five kids could be seen on his back taking a ride around the pasture.

When Rock died a few years later, I didn't have the heart to tell the kids I had sold the carcass to the knacker. I told them I had buried him...as if I would dig a hole through southern Idaho hardpan big enough to hold a 2,000-pound horse. I was just too softhearted. Apart from the chickens, which Betty killed, nothing "died" on our farm. Cats and dogs might "run away," but they never got hit by cars. Even our calf had "run away." The kids never asked about the fresh meat that happened to appear at the same time, and I never volunteered any extra information.

A few other animals deserve honorable mention. Terry was prone to bringing home birds with broken wings. I don't think any of them survived. One spring, Bill and Terry robbed the pigeon nests in the bell tower of the local cemetery. Terry was convinced that if he raised them, they would come home when released. Once freed, they did stay around for a few weeks, but then returned to the flock at the cemetery.

The funniest pets he had, if you can call them pets, were tadpoles. He and Bill had caught them in a nearby irrigation ditch. Terry had a shallow plastic dish designed for turtles that he used for his tadpoles. There was a log and fresh grass prepared for their transition into froghood. Every day he checked to see how their legs were growing. One afternoon he ran home from the school bus to check on their development. They had all disappeared. Little balls of lint could be seen hopping all over the house. It was like one of the plagues of Egypt. Tiny frogs seemed to be everywhere. They had all hopped out of the turtle dish. Betty was not impressed. The frogs needed a new home. Terry decided to build a little pond. He sunk a large pot into the ground in the pasture behind the house. The top lip of the pot was at ground level with the dirt patted and smoothed to give it the look of a miniature swimming pool. The pot was then filled with water and the frogs were transferred to their new home. We still had Bossy, our little Jersey cow, at the time. She had taken great interest in all the activity taking place in her pasture. When Terry stepped back to observe his creation, Bossy stepped forward for a closer look. She took a sniff, immersed her muzzle in the pot, and sucked up the entire contents.

Chapter Notes

[1]Crow hopping is a mild form of bucking where a horse arches its back and takes short stiff hops with all four feet coming off the ground.

THE STORIES OF MY FATHER

GOOD OL' COUNTRY FOLK

INTERESTING PEOPLE LIVE in the country. We shared a party line with the neighbors. That meant that our phones were all connected. Each family had its own "ring." Ours was a long-short, "riiiiiiing-ring...riiiiiiing-ring." Anyone on the line could pick up and listen, so you needed to be careful what you said. Ruth Sailor's chief form of recreation was listening in to other people's calls. I often heard a muffled, "Quiet Henry, I can't hear," while talking to someone on the phone. Henry's recreation was shooting other people's cats and dogs. We eventually bought their place and were happy to see them move.

A Seventh-day Adventist family named Smith lived about a quarter mile up the hill from us. Their recreation seemed to be religion, and they kept to themselves. Their goats were in our yard eating the shrubs just about every Saturday. The Smiths wouldn't retrieve their animals until after sunset when their Sabbath ended. It was a bit of an irritant and not a good promotion for their church.

Myrtle and Harry Sloan lived across the road from the Smiths. Betty occasionally walked up the hill for coffee with Myrtle. Myrtle entertained herself by complaining about Harry. Their little boy and Terry loved to wrestle. One time the boys wanted to see what would happen if they dropped a kitten into Myrtle's wringer washing machine. Well, that was a sad lesson. I never quite trusted Harry after finding that he occupied himself by watching the rest of us with his binoculars. Poor Betty, keep in mind she was in her early twenties, had taken to tanning in the nude. After all, we lived five miles out of town. Who was going to see?

Our favorite neighbors were Pio and Phyllis Fenicottero. They lived just a couple hundred yards up the road from us. Pio worked for the local power company. He was an Italian whose first order of business after buying the farm was to plant a vineyard. The second order was to build a wine cellar. They had three girls, Rosie, Susie, and Trina. We often got together to "sample" Pio's latest vintage and play cards. They were a fun couple.

An old German couple, Klaus and Mary Reimers, lived about two miles further down the road. Klaus was about the age Betty's dad would have been and was a great support. He loved fishing and often dropped off a burlap bag of crappies or blue gills. It was a nice gesture, but I suspect he liked fishing but didn't like fish. Those little fish, with the sharp spines of their fins and tough scales, were murder to clean.

We often visited the Reimers. They were almost like grandparents to Terry, Vicki, and Liz. One Saturday evening Mary served boysenberry pie. Vicki was quite concerned that we were eating "poison" berry pie. She didn't want to die but couldn't resist fresh pie and ice cream. Terry was concerned that Klaus didn't attend church and had to ask why. Klaus answered, "I try it once." He pointed out the window and continued, "Zat afternoon I was sitting under zat tree over zere cleaning fish. A bolt of lightning hit ze tree. Heiliger Strohsak! *Holy smokes!* Ze Devil was warning me about going to church, and I promise zat I never do it again!"

As evening came on, a huge flock of ducks landed in Klaus's corn patch. Our farms happened to be in the Pacific Flyway, and we could count on thousands of ducks and geese coming through every year. They can do a lot of damage to any corn or grain still standing. Klaus pulled a pump shotgun from behind the kitchen door and asked me to come outside. We walked to the corn patch. You couldn't see anything, but it sounded like the ducks were having a convention. What a racket! Klaus aimed at a thirty-degree angle toward the ground and fired off a shot. The whistling, quacking, and squawking increased at least fifty decibels as the flock took to the air. Klaus raised his shotgun to eye level and fired again. He pumped in a third shell, raised his gun another thirty degrees, and shot another round. He nudged me and said, "Come tomorrow morning before you go to church and I have some ducks for you."

Early Sunday morning, I milked the cow, checked the feed and water for the chickens, and then drove out to the Reimers. Klaus was waiting with a fresh cup of coffee. We walked to the corn patch and began picking up ducks. Now this was my kind of hunting. Suddenly Klaus swore, "Mist! Was machst du den hier?" *Damn! What are you doing here?* A yearling heifer lay dead on the ground. She had been standing in the corn the night before. I told Klaus I would come back in the afternoon to help with the butchering. Maybe that wasn't the best way to hunt ducks after all. Speaking of which, we picked up eleven dead ducks and one dead calf.

THE STORIES OF MY FATHER

RUSSIAN 7.62

FUDGING ON HUNTING regulations was never an issue for me. Like my dad, I felt there was a difference between what was moral and what was legal. If we needed the meat, poaching was simply God's way of providing. Living on the farm in the middle of pheasant country offered plenty of "God's provision."

The first order of business was to purchase a shotgun. I had never owned one and settled on a 16-gauge bolt action Marlin. It didn't kick as hard as a 12 gauge but had enough power to handle most game birds. I could hardly wait to try it out! On my way home with my brand-new shotgun and several boxes of shells, I came across three nice pheasant cocks. I skidded to a stop in the middle of the road, jumped out of the car, and jammed three shells into the magazine. I was so excited that I couldn't hold the barrel still but aimed as best I could as I jacked one bullet after another out of the gun. I heard an "ahem" and turned around to see Jake Scott, the local game warden, standing right behind me. I hadn't heard him pull up, but there he was, arms crossed and an accusing glare in his eyes. *Holy cow! No*

hunting license; out of season; and shooting from the
middle of the road. Crap! What was I thinking?

Jake slowly shifted his gaze to my feet. I looked down
to see three unspent shotgun shells. I had emptied the gun
but hadn't fired a shot. Thank God for the worst case of
"buck fever" I ever experienced. I looked up, smiled, and
said, "Just testing you."

More lessons were yet to come. Grandma Baker
always kept a loaded gun beside her kitchen door. I kept my
shotgun and .22 loaded and hanging on a gun rack near the
back door. You never knew when a pheasant might land
beside the house. I found out that you also never know what
goes through the minds of little boys. I came home one day
to find that Terry and Bill had been chasing each other
through the house with the guns. Their cop and robber game
could have easily turned tragic. Lesson learned!

That fall Lee wanted to take me hunting in the
mountains near Council, Idaho. I needed a rifle and settled
on a service model Russian 7.62, known by many hunters as
a Russian .30-06. Being military surplus, it was affordable.
I didn't have money for a scope, but that particular rifle was
about six inches longer than the standard hunting rifle. Even
using the iron sights, it was deadly accurate. In fact, it was
the rifle of choice for Russian snipers. I immediately
sporterized the heavy military stock. With a lot of sanding, a
fresh wood stain, and re-bluing of the barrel, I had a
beautiful rifle. The local stores didn't carry the ammunition,
but I found a guy who had the dies for handloading. This
posed a problem a few times and eventually blew up the gun,
but more on that later.

The hunting party consisted of me and Terry, Lee
and Bill, and a friend named Charlie Butler. We used
packhorses to follow trails used by Basque shepherds earlier
in the year. What a trip! Terry was nine or ten years old, too
young to hunt, but eager to come along. It was beautiful

country with lots of game and natural hot springs for bathing at night. Unfortunately, the packhorse I was leading shied when a grouse burst out of the brush. The horse slid down the side of a ravine and took me with it. If I had let go, we would have lost the horse and gear. Later in the day, we tethered the horses and split up to stalk game. Terry was a great little companion. He knew to keep quiet and was a good spotter. Unfortunately, that day I was not a good shooter. I had ample opportunities but couldn't hit the side of a barn.

After a frustrating day, I decided I needed some target practice. At twenty-five yards I was barely on the target, let alone anywhere near the bullseye. When I went over the bank with that horse, the front gun sight had struck a tree. At a hundred yards, my shots would have been off by close to two feet. Only other hunters will relate to the sick feeling I had. Lee, Bill, and Charlie had no luck. Their problem, in my opinion, was too much talk, the occasional cigarette, and Skoal chewing tobacco. Mule deer have big ears and good noses.

Charlie Butler was a funny guy. He had served in the Korean War and later adopted a couple little Korean boys. He kept telling us how those little boys had told him, "Daddy, get us a bear." He had tons of experience hunting and trapping and would have done fine on his own. He was a great storyteller and loved to tease. The first morning he told the boys that they had been talking to each other in their sleep. Of course, they wanted to hear more. He related a conversation between Bill and Terry that went like this:

"Fish...fiish...fiiiish."

"Where?"

"Over there...."

"Where?"

"Over theeeere...."

"You fool! You broke your pole!"

Terry asked Charlie, "Did we really say that?" Charlie grinned and said, "Well what do you think?"

For some people hunting is more about camp life than bagging game. It's stories and pranks, camp coffee in the mornings and beer at night. I had stuck in a spare pack of Marlboros, anticipating that Lee would run out of cigarettes. He did, but I let him suffer and whine for about half a day before pulling it out. He was fuming in more ways than one when he realized I had them all along.

The other hunting trip of memory was with Terry and Buzz Boemer. We took Buzz's old Chevy flatbed truck. It had a military-style canvas back for sleeping. Typically, Buzz spent the week before a trip trying to get the truck to run. After arriving at a base camp, he spent the next few days working on his truck so we could get home. You have to be a guy to understand the special relationship between a man and his truck.

This trip took us into the Owyhee County wilderness of southwestern Idaho. It was fairly open desert country with rolling hills, ravines, and sparse vegetation. The whitetail deer had over-populated and a special hunt had been opened. Buzz and I were to set up a base camp. Our wives, Betty and Beverly, and two or three other couples would come two days later. Problems with Buzz's truck ensured that we arrived late at night. In the dark, we didn't see a hunting camp that was about a hundred yards from our spot. There were probably eight or ten people there. That's a close concentration of a lot of firepower.

The first morning, Terry and I hunted while Buzz spent time working on the truck. We stuck to the ridges as much as possible. I remember passing a small cave, more like a large bear den, as we peered down at the creeks and water holes. Holy cow! There seemed to be deer everywhere. I had no problem getting my first little buck. By the time the larger group arrived, Buzz and I had our deer. Another was hanging, waiting to be tagged. We figured we could easily fill everyone's tags. We figured wrong.

The group arrived in the late afternoon of the second day, too late to do any hunting. The following morning, just as we were finishing breakfast, a herd of fourteen deer ran between our camp and the neighboring camp. People were grabbing their guns and wildly shooting as the deer passed through. It was a regular shooting gallery. We might as well have been aiming at each other. Some people were screaming and running for cover. Finally, the shooting stopped and the dust cleared. Faces began appearing from behind rocks and trucks. It was a miracle that no people or vehicles were hit. Ironically, no deer were hit either.

Terry, Betty, and I went out on our own. Betty loved hunting and fishing but was usually tied up looking after kids. I thought this would be a treat for her but once again, I thought wrong. We were over a mile from camp when a terrible blizzard hit. Visibility was near zero. Your own tracks disappeared in just minutes. Because I had been there the day before, I was able to make out the odd landmark as we struggled to get back to camp. We passed about ten yards from the cave I had seen on that first day out. If we had only known, a woman from the other camp had lost her way and was huddled inside. They found her frozen body three days later.

At the camp, everyone was clustered in the back of Buzz's truck. Buzz pulled out a bottle of Jack Daniel's and passed it around to warm everybody up. I handed the bottle to Terry to see what he would do. The little shit looked at it, took a big drink, and gasped. He then passed it to the next person as though he did it all the time. Not bad for an eleven-year-old. The decision was made to drive out caravan-style while we still could. It was blowing so bad, no one was willing to bring in the extra deer that was still hanging. In disgust, Betty flung the flap open on the back of the truck and went to get it. She was hoping to shoot her own deer and didn't want to use up her tag. Of course, everyone wanted a share of the meat. As we drove out, I wondered why the neighboring camp did not fall in behind us. I found out a few days later.

The bolt action rifles weren't designed for left-handers like myself and I decided to sell the Russian 7.62. Getting good hand loads for it had been a challenge. Only seasoned hunters who hand load will understand some of the issues. Sometimes the bullets weren't seated properly. I mean, you really shouldn't be able to pull a slug out of a cartridge with your fingers or see it hit the ground halfway to the target. Occasionally a reloader will forget to put the powder in a cartridge. When the primer goes off, the bullet travels a few inches down the barrel and stops. If you were to jack in another cartridge and fire, the barrel would split and anyone standing nearby could be seriously injured. I was ready for a newer rifle.

I sold the 7.62 to a work buddy. I don't know what exactly happened, but it blew up while he was at the shooting range. It may have been caused by an old shell that had been reloaded too many times. It may have been caused by a faulty load. He may have accidentally shot a bullet that wasn't designed for the gun. At any rate, when he pulled the trigger, the side of the firing chamber blew out and a piece of metal took off the bottom half of his right ear. He was lucky not to lose an eye or worse.

SMALL TOWN BLUES

GRACE METALIOUS SHOULD have visited Payette before she wrote *Peyton Place*. Her book has themes of hypocrisy, social inequities, incest, abortion, adultery, and murder[1]. Payette had all those things plus a strong presence of the Ku Klux Klan[2]. The Grand Master of the Klan west of the Mississippi lived in Payette. He once emphatically stated, "Never will a n... sleep overnight in Payette County." Betty and I did not share those sympathies, but looking back, I only remember one black family ever coming into town. They were gone the next morning. Payette had one Jewish family and a few dozen Catholics. A couple Mexican families lived outside the city limits.

We were slowly working our way into the middle class. I was earning about $4,800 a year, not a bad income in the early 1960s. A friend of Mom's named Goldie approached me and asked if I would consider a job as her husband's personal secretary. Goldie and Jack Marshall owned the Marshall Company. I had worked there for about a year when we first moved back to Payette from The Dalles. I told Goldie that she couldn't afford me. She said, "We can start you at $10,000 a year." I responded, "When do I start?"

The first order of business was getting my typing up to forty words per minute. The second was getting to forty words per minute without mistakes. Jack dictated three to four letters every day. I edited and typed the letters and placed them on his desk. The following day the letters would be back in my "to do" bin with all the mistakes circled. I would then retype and resubmit the correspondence to Jack. This went on for several weeks. I happened to be in a management meeting in Jack's office and saw a stack of my letters in the wastebasket. He hadn't mailed a single letter. Jack looked at me and said, "Sorry Gary, but you have to admit, you've finally learned how to type. Now we can get to work."

As part of my training, Jack regularly sent me through the shop. I checked inventories and job orders, and I sometimes chatted with our foreman. One day while passing through, I leaned into a large cart of lumber to help move it from the warehouse. The axel snapped on the cart and the load collapsed on me, crushing the fused discs in my back. The second surgery was much more complex than the first. I mention it because it would later come back to haunt me.

A quick aside regarding hospitals. I've probably spent more time than the average person convalescing in hospital beds. I've had surgery for my shoulder, twice for my back, twice for hernias, plus day surgeries for less serious injuries. Constipation has been a problem my whole life. They usually want you cleaned out for medical procedures, which often meant enemas. I had one of note. The nurse had done her part and told me to leave the table and use the bathroom, which was about ten feet away. I told her that I couldn't hold it that far. She assured me that patients made it all the time. I lost my load about halfway and then locked myself in the bathroom. I was so embarrassed. It took two hours to talk me out. The nurse assured me that everything had been cleaned up and there were no hurt feelings, that these things sometimes happened. In later hospital stays, I sometimes spent an hour or more sitting on the toilet doing my best to squeeze anything out, and then refusing to flush until I could show the nurse. I would do almost anything to avoid an enema.

Back on the job, I learned how to run the office, manage the floor, and work with the sales people. I saw how the trucks were loaded and what was required to install the heavy oak pews. Jack was treating me like an assistant manager. Toward the end of my second year, he suffered a heart attack while on a business trip to Germany. Suddenly all that training came in handy. I started walking the plant floor and analyzing the productivity. I immediately recognized how to produce the same output with fewer men. I cut the staff from 35 to 13, and we increased both productivity and profitability.

Getting the older men to change their habits was a challenge. They saw me as a "youngster" that belonged in the office behind a typewriter. Things came to a head one day when walking the floor. I stopped to watch Mort Bradley on the sander and, for probably the fifth time, insisted he change the way he operated the machine. He knocked the clipboard out of my hand and came at me with both fists. The fight was on. I knew if I backed down, I would never keep the respect of the men. The boxing skills of my teenage years were of little use in what became an all-out brawl. The men gathered around, afraid to root one way or the other. Mort was a big man, but I matched him blow for blow. The fight ended when we wrestled each other to the ground, totally spent. Mort never became a friend, but I gained his respect, and he didn't question my orders afterward. Lee was driving truck and doing installations for Marshall's. He was in the plant that day and stood with the crowd. Here was a man I looked up to; he was married to my mother; we had hunted and fished together; but he did not stand up for me, this time or any other that I recall. He could have stepped in and stopped the fight but didn't. That hurt me more than any of Mort's punches.

When Jack returned to work, he noticed right away that we were missing over half the crew. I explained the changes I had made, how many men had been released, and how we had increased production. Jack took me to the office and asked me to sit down. He was concerned that I had overstepped my authority. He told me to rehire all the men I had let go. I explained that we didn't need them, in fact, the company was more profitable without them. He countered that the company might not need them, but they needed the company. Red Simons was a case in point. He was an older man with six or seven kids still at home. He supported the local Catholic Church and served the local community as a dedicated Boy Scout leader. There was no place for him to go in a small town like Payette. Jack explained that he and Margo didn't need the company. It existed to provide jobs for the community. If I was really concerned about productivity, I should increase the sales staff and bring in more work. In Jack's mind, the needs of people were more important than the bottom line.

With the money I was earning at Marshall's, we moved from the farm to a nice home across the street from the high school and just half a block from an elementary school. The move was a major step up from the farm. The house included a full basement and an upstairs rental suite. It was perfect for the kids and they quickly adjusted. The pets didn't fare so well. Tom quickly made his way back the farm; Lady was killed by a car; and Dinah was soon back in a cast, also a victim of local traffic. This time I was more honest with the kids. They refused to stop looking for Lady until I told them the truth.

We decided it was time to get serious about church.

Early in our marriage we attended the Pentecostal Church with questionable results and had drifted away while on the farm. My mother was looking for a church at the same time. She felt that church would be beneficial for my half-brother, Bill. It had to be a church that allowed for their family life-style, notably Lee's smoking and their mutual enjoyment of social drinking and occasional dancing. It seemed the Catholic Church was the only choice. If Mom thought the church would bring Bill into line, she was sorely wrong. Once, when at her wit's end, she glared at him and said, "Do you want to go to hell when you die?" He quickly responded, "I want to go wherever Daddy goes." Lee was definitely not on track to the Pearly Gates.

For our family, it was a good choice. Betty found the spiritual connection she had been missing. Vicki and Liz fit in. Terry was soon serving as an altar boy and a member of the church Scout troop. I found it more difficult. Father Halpin was the most patient, loving pastor I've ever met, but between my "sins and faults of youth" and the beliefs and non-beliefs of my parents, I had a hard time making the transition. My first confession went on for two hours before Father Halpin cut it short. I think he had heard all he could take and figured that God could fill in the blanks. I was in the middle of my second time through membership classes when Father Halpin told me to just come to church with my family, that my questions would be answered in God's own time. I did enjoy the church and was an active volunteer in building their new gymnasium. Father Halpin became a trusted friend and mentor for our family. Imagine this, he was concerned that I was depriving my family by giving too much money to the church. I told him that if ten percent was good enough for the Bible, it was good enough for me.

We had serious marital problems from time to time over the years. The move did not fix things. One of my regrets is that we didn't do more as a family. I was obsessed with work. The only family vacation I remember was a road trip to the Oregon coast. Jack had loaned me his Cadillac and insisted I take some time off. We visited the Oregon Caves and Crater Lake. Along the coast, we collected rocks at Agate Beach and visited the Sea Lion Caves. It was too little, too late. In the meantime, Betty's mom had invested in several tourist cabins just outside Tillamook, Oregon. Betty began taking the kids there for several weeks in the summer. I stayed home and went to the plant every day. Our marriage was in trouble.

Betty is no longer alive to tell her side of the story and I take much of the blame. We were teenagers when we married; we had totally different backgrounds; and we had less than ideal parental support. Betty gave birth to five children in eight years before I went for the vasectomy. We shouldn't have married in the first place. The move to town could have been a blessing but proved otherwise.

Divorce seemed to be in the air. Mom and Lee divorced. Norm and Carla had problems that eventually led to a split. Buzz and Beverly had a horrendous break-up. They lived on a farm on the west side of town. Buzz came home early one day to find a stranger in bed with Beverly. Before the guy ran out of the house, Buzz shot him in the thigh with a 12-gauge shotgun. Buzz was charged with attempted murder. In the trial that followed, he was found not guilty. The jury was composed of farmers and ranchers from around the area. They interpreted the event as a man protecting his property and secretly wished Buzz had aimed a little higher. A few thought he'd shot the wrong person. One by one our support group was eroding away.

The biggest factor keeping us together was our children. Betty was having a hard time emotionally and fearful that I might take away the kids. I came home from work one afternoon to find an empty house. Betty was gone; the kids were gone; their clothes were gone; and there was no note. I contacted the police. Well into the second week, I received a bill for a power hook-up at an address on the other side of town. Forest Cochrane, an old high school buddy that worked in the post office, had noticed Betty's name on the envelope and forwarded it to me. I contacted the sheriff and followed him to a small garage apartment. Harsh words were exchanged as the sheriff escorted the kids to my car. A few days later Betty returned. She wasn't leaving without her children. The writing was on the wall, but we weren't ready to read it.

Leading up to this, the young family renting our apartment were having serious problems. Nick and Jolene had probably been married for about two years. Jolene was a vivacious little redhead. Nick was a big muscular guy. He had a scar running down his forehead and across his nose from having smashed through a windshield in a car accident. Nick was not someone you wanted to cross. They had a little girl and all the potential of being a happy little family. Unfortunately, potential and reality often don't come together. They were struggling, and I made the mistake of getting involved with Jolene. Payette is a small community and rumors immediately began flying. Even Father Halpin, possibly as a result of someone's confession, got involved. *You can't tell me that everything said in the confessional stays in the confessional!* He recognized me and Jolene as we were taking a drive to Ontario. That priest drove up beside us and forced me off the road. He was angry at what he saw happening to our families and in his strong Irish brogue let us know in no uncertain terms how foolish and selfish we were.

Betty and I decided to sell the house and move to a recently vacated estate known locally as The Country Club. Fountains graced the front circular drive. Each bedroom in the main building had its own fireplace. The bar had been stocked by celebrity patrons who came for the fall pheasant hunting. A few empty bottles labeled with well-known Hollywood names were still on the shelves. A small house stood behind the club where the caretaker and his wife had lived. The grounds included a chicken barn that had provided the freshest and possibly the best fried chicken in the country. I envisioned a beautiful home in which to raise the kids. Betty wanted to reopen the club. We were both excited about the move but could not agree on the future.

I was still involved with Jolene and a separation seemed inevitable. One evening Betty handed me a .22 pistol saying, "You'll need this." Whether it was from a premonition or something she had heard from friends, I don't know. I will ever be grateful that she was concerned for me, if not for herself, then for the kids. Late at night a couple weeks later, a car pulled up behind me as I was driving home. It kept pulling up to my rear bumper, flashing its high beams. I was forced to stop the car.

Looking in the rear-view mirror, I saw Nick get out of the driver's side. Three of his friends followed, each carrying a baseball bat. I rolled down my window. Nick folded his arms and rested them on the window base. Our faces were only inches apart. I slowly raised my hand and placed the barrel of the pistol against his forehead, "Tell your friends to get back in the car. You follow them. If you turn around, I'll blow your head off."

Not long after, Betty raised the subject of Jolene and said, "Get her out of town! Her husband is on his way to kill her." I contacted Jolene and arranged to drive her and her little girl to her parents' home. This might have been the chance to make things right with Betty, but so much had happened. Jolene and I were thirty or forty miles out of Payette when we had a blowout. When I opened the trunk, I found that Betty had packed my clothes and personal belongings. There was no turning back. I phoned Jack to say I was quitting my job with the Marshall Company. He begged me to reconsider, that we could make it work. I couldn't see myself staying in Payette. Too much had happened there, and it didn't seem like a safe place for me and Jolene. Without the job I couldn't make the payments on The Country Club. Betty was soon out of a home and without means to look after the children. The kids moved in with me, but only for a short stay before Betty showed up with a U-Haul trailer. I was adamant that the children weren't going anywhere. We were very nearly into a fistfight when the door to Terry's room swung open. The poor boy was on his knees beside his bed holding his rosary, sobbing through a Hail Mary. That ended the argument. An hour later Betty was driving back to Payette with the children in the back seat of the car and the U-Haul trailing behind.

Divorce is a terrible thing. Family and friends begin taking sides. They say blood is thicker than water. My Mom was fearful that Betty would move to Oregon and she would lose contact with her grandchildren. Because I had managed Marshall's, had been a member of the Lion's Club, and dealt with various lawyers in real estate deals, I held all the cards when it came to child custody. My lawyer put together a case against Betty and we prepared for court. I will never forget that day. The old oak court benches were well worn from the fears and tears of cases past. Betty and the three children, Terry, Vicki, and Liz were seated in the second row. They were all in tears. The little girls were trembling. Betty must have known that she didn't have a chance to leave the courtroom with her kids, but she would fight to the bitter end. I took one look and my heart melted. I couldn't do it. I took my lawyer aside. He told me not to be a fool. Custody was virtually a formality. I would get everything I wanted. I dropped my case. There had to be a better way.

I managed a down payment on a small older home on North 8th Street just off 7th Avenue where it crosses the railroad tracks. My hope was that Betty would manage the payments and the children would continue in their school. That didn't last long. Betty was commuting to Ontario every day to work, and there was little help coming from the community. She soon moved to Ontario and shortly after that to Woodburn, Oregon south of Portland.

Chapter Notes

[1]Shortly after an elderly woman was stabbed to death in Payette, Gary's younger brother, Bill, brought home a blood-smeared butcher knife claiming it had been used in the crime. Gary's mother, Wanda, thought Bill was pranking her, hid the knife away, and forgot about it. Several weeks later, she had second thoughts and contacted the police. The knife led to the conviction of an older teenager.

[2]Gary made these comments a number of times, even naming the Grand Master and an informant that had given Klan membership files to the FBI.

BACHELOR DAD

AFTER A FEW SHORT-TERM jobs, Jolene and I moved to Salem, Oregon. We married, but it didn't last long. Finding myself with no family responsibilities, life seemed pointless. A man needs his family. I started shifting from job to job, drinking and fighting, wrecking cars. One day the phone rang. Betty wanted to talk about Terry. He was fifteen and just about to enter his sophomore year of high school. According to Betty, Terry was concerned for me, thought I needed someone, and asked if he could live with me. According to Terry, Betty had approached him and asked if he would like to live with his dad. I said yes and immediately began getting my life back in order. With all the trouble I had been into in Salem, I decided it best to head for the hills. I picked up Terry and we drove to Valsetz, Oregon.

Valsetz was founded at the end of World War I when a spur of the Valley and Siletz Railroad was built to accommodate the William W. Mitchell lumber company. As small and isolated as it was, it had a national reputation for record precipitation – up to twelve feet (144 inches) of rain per year – and a newspaper, the *Valsetz Star*, which had been started by nine-year-old Dorothy Ann Hobson in the 1930s. Winter weather was such that it sometimes snowed as much as three feet or more one night and had bare wet ground the next.

When we arrived, Valsetz was owned by the Boise Cascade Corporation. When I say owned, I mean everything: houses, streets, school, store, bunkhouses – everything. While waiting for a company house, we moved into the company bunkhouse. The rules allowed no eating or drinking in the bunkhouse, which meant going to the restaurant every day for every meal. It was a pretty good set up for the restaurant operator. He also ran the only store, the two gas pumps, and a two-lane bowling alley. It was rumored (and probably true) that when food passed its expiration date in the store, it was cooked and served in the restaurant. The town also included a post office, an elementary school, a high school, and a small Catholic Church building. The old growth timber ran out in the 1970s and the town was dismantled in 1984.

Terry and I arrived just as the football season was beginning at Valsetz High School in 1965. The school had only 35 students of which, with Terry included, there were only 10 boys. That league played eight-man football. The team was so desperate that Terry played his first game before attending a practice. I worked my first shift turning plywood sheets that night. We were both nearly incapacitated the following day. He wasn't in shape and I hadn't done manual labor for years.

Once we moved into a company house, I managed to get a small oil stove to keep off the chill and a combination wood-electric stove for the kitchen. The house was never warm. A table and two chairs were acquired for the kitchen and an old sofa for the living room. We had no television. We had two bedrooms, but only one bed. I worked the graveyard shift and slept during the day. Terry had the bed at night.

We were only there a few weeks when Buzz Boemer showed up. He needed someplace to "disappear" for a while. You can't survive in a place like Valsetz without a sense of humor. Charlie Benson, our foreman, hired Buzz on the spot and drove him to the sawdust pile to introduce him to his new job. When Buzz asked just what he would be doing, Charlie replied, "Oh, just eating sawdust and shitting presto-logs." They then drove back to the mill and Buzz was shown his place on the line. We still had only one bed. Buzz went on the swing shift, 4:00 p.m. to midnight. I was working midnight to 7:00 a.m. Terry was going to school during the day. The bed was occupied pretty well twenty-four hours a day.

Those were lean times. Having grown up in the '30s and '40s, I would not waste a thing. I scorched a large pot of spaghetti and insisted that we would not throw any out but would eat every noodle. About the third day of burnt tasting spaghetti, I caught Terry feeding the leftovers to the dog. Terry spent much of his spare time hunting and fishing. He didn't do that well. In the time we were there, I remember him bringing home one deer, a duck, and a pigeon. I don't remember any fish. A half pigeon each doesn't make for a very filling meal. We made up for that midwinter at a community turkey shoot. There were no guns, just bingo cards. Terry won the first turkey and I won the next two. I gave mine away.

Terry, in many ways raised himself. He didn't have an allowance, so he worked hand setting pins at the bowling alley on the weekends. He served as altar boy in our little Catholic Church. Father McCrea drove in once or twice a month to take confessions and conduct Mass. He didn't like the trip and the weather didn't have to be very bad before he would cancel the service. We rarely saw Father in the winter. I sometimes took off on weekends, leaving Terry to fend for himself. He was a good kid but was still a kid. One weekend while I was gone, he hosted a house party. I wouldn't have known, but my first morning back, I was getting dressed and glanced out the bedroom window. The yard was strewn with beer cans and the odd whiskey bottle. I turned to Terry and asked, "Was anyone drinking here while I was gone?" He knew I wouldn't ask if I didn't already know and replied, "Well, Jim and I had a couple beers." The night of the party there was about two feet of snow. Two days later there was none. I guess the kids thought, "out of sight, out of mind." Nothing more was said and so far as I know, no more parties occurred at our house.

We had a sheriff, Tim Franklin. He was a large, heavy man that provided more of a presence than actual work. The few times he tried to run down teenagers that were drinking or prowling around, the kids simply ran into the woods and hid. Tim couldn't run fast enough to catch anyone. Sometimes on the weekends he left town so he wouldn't have to. Come Monday he would visit his contacts, find out what had gone on, and then phone various parents. He phoned me on the Tuesday after the party. His intent was to maintain a semblance of stability without getting anyone into serious trouble. For the most part, this worked well for our little town. Small communities have their own way of looking after each other.

We had been in Valsetz about three months when Vicki joined us. She had taken our divorce much harder than Terry and Liz, and she was becoming unmanageable for Betty. I quickly acquired another bed and we set up the second bedroom. Valsetz was a good place for her, but we weren't there much longer.

The manual labor caught up with me. I had a hernia (my second) shortly after starting work in the mill. It healed quickly, and I was soon back to work but in less than six months my old back injury forced us down the mountain.

All the stooping and twisting required in the mill gradually caused my second surgery to deteriorate. I was soon facing several years of court hearings, doctors' testimonies, and hard times as I tried to collect compensation. The insurance company wanted a quick settlement and insisted on another surgery. Their doctor testified that he could make me as good as new...with the stipulation that I might end up in a wheelchair and would definitely lose much of my mobility. I was in a lot of pain, but I could walk, sit, and bend over. It seemed to me that apart from possible pain relief, I would be worse off after surgery and my doctor agreed. After several years of legal maneuvering I was forced to take a settlement. During that time period we moved back to Idaho. It had to be hard for Terry and Vicki. In the space of two years they attended school in five towns: Woodburn, Valsetz, Fruitland, Weiser, and Boise. I would sometimes hold a job for a couple months, but just couldn't manage the pain.

My mom and youngest brother, Bill, joined us in a little two-story house in Boise. That didn't last. Bill was 16 or 17 and always into one thing or another. After their first month with us, I received a phone bill for almost two hundred dollars. Bill had been maintaining a long-distant relationship with a girlfriend. I phoned Bell Telephone and told them to come get their phone. They refused because of the unpaid bill. I told them if they wouldn't come to the house, they could pick it up in the yard. They came for the phone. Mom wanted help with Bill. I needed help with Vicki. I was unemployed and my compensation checks were often delayed or withheld while the lawyers haggled over my claim. Mom finally moved.

Without Mom's help with the rent, I couldn't keep the house, so we moved to a small house next to the Boise auction barn. It was a definite step down. The house was set on cinderblocks and had practically no insulation. It had been placed there from somewhere else in the city. The yard was bare clay; nothing would grow except a small tuft of grass where a horse had dropped a pile of road apples.

If it hadn't been for Terry, we wouldn't have had a car. He worked every summer and part-time through the school year to pay the payments on a 1957 Volkswagen Beetle. I used it as much as he did. The brakes needed constant adjustment. One time I pulled into someone's driveway and coasted through their garage door and into the back wall. I felt terrible...mentally and physically. I was depressed, in constant pain, and high on painkillers much of the time. I managed to get the car repaired but soon after was given a ticket for driving without a license. At that time in Idaho, any traffic violation required that you go to day court. I was called before the judge and issued a ten-dollar ticket. I told the judge that I was unemployed, that the car belonged to my son, and that I didn't have ten dollars. I asked for jail time, better to be sitting in jail than sitting at home. The judge glared at me, tore up the ticket, and said, "If you can't afford ten dollars, you can't afford to drive. Now get out of here."

On the home front, Vicki was one unhappy girl. She refused to walk to school, so I began walking with her. I would wait at the front of the school till she entered the building. She would walk through the front door, down the hall, and out the back door. I wouldn't see her again until supper time or later. She had a few friends, but not the kind I could approve of. I suspect her friends' parents felt the same way but what can you do? Believe me, I tried. I counseled with a fundamentalist minister. His understanding of child psychology was insulting. You can't just accuse a thirteen-year-old of secret sins for which there is no evidence and demand repentance and obedience.

All Vicki's childhood she had wanted a horse. I thought maybe that would capture her attention. I found an older American Saddlebred named Jasper. He was a beautiful chestnut with chromed mane and tail. In his prime he had been a five-gaited show horse. The breed has bloodlines going back to the Revolutionary War. He still had plenty of energy and immediately reverted to his show stance as soon as a rider mounted. He was the perfect horse for a spunky little blonde, just not my spunky little blonde. Vicki showed no interest. There was no point in keeping him.

The day came when Vicki didn't come home from school and couldn't be found. Terry and I knelt by the bed and prayed that God would bring her home. I promised God I would do whatever I needed to, if He would only hear. Three days later, Terry came rushing home in the middle of the school day. The police had contacted him and asked that he be there when they came to the house. They had found Vicki. She and a girlfriend had gone on a joyride with a couple older guys. There had been a terrible accident. Her little girlfriend, Cindy, had died. We knew the family. Feelings were such that I did not attend the funeral. Vicki moved back to her mom's in Portland.

During those years, I had other worries involving Terry. The United States was stepping up the war in Vietnam and had reintroduced the draft. Over the next few years, my youngest brother, Bill Grimes, joined the Navy. Terry's cousins, Pat and Mike Grimes, both joined the U.S Army. Dave Barnes, a cousin on his mom's side, also joined the Army. Pat and Dave would both see active duty in Vietnam. When Terry turned seventeen, he asked if I would sign him into the Navy Reserve. I told him to check it out and we could talk. He immediately visited the local Marine, Army, and Navy recruiters. The Navy promised that if he finished high school, they would sponsor him for college and officer training. I breathed a sigh of relief.

About that time, my dad introduced Terry to a Bible

correspondence course. Of the whole family, Terry had always been the most church oriented. For years he had wanted to become a Catholic priest. In fact, he had obtained church sponsorship and been accepted to the minor seminary in Mount Angel, Oregon just weeks before moving in with me. I don't know what changed his mind. Now he was again fascinated with the Bible and started looking into various churches. The two of us invited the Mormon elders to the house with their introductory course. Their sincerity alone was very convincing. The services were dynamic. However, the second or third service we attended was a "Fast and Testimony" service. Terry was shocked to see a couple guys he knew from school stand up and publicly repent of their smoking and drinking. They were crying. Their mothers were crying and hugging their boys. We left as soon as we could. This wasn't the way things were done in the Catholic Church.

I told Terry to write the authors of his Bible correspondence course and ask them about the Mormons. About three months later, long enough that Terry had forgotten about the letter, a pastor and his assistant came to the house. Fred Coulter pastored a church in Salt Lake City, Utah and looked after a small group in Boise. It was the first we realized that a church was associated with the Bible course Terry had been receiving. The church was known as The Radio Church of God and had been founded by Herbert W. Armstrong. Mr. Armstrong and his son, Garner Ted Armstrong, had weekly radio broadcasts around the world. I attended a couple services with Terry. The congregation was very loving and immediately accepted him as one of their own. It seemed like a good place for him at the time. My back was gradually healing, and I was occasionally accompanying a long-haul trucker that lived next door. A church family named Green opened their door to Terry during my trips.

Terry was becoming somewhat fanatical. He decided that we could no longer eat pork or shellfish. I served the last of our pork and beans one night, and he refused to eat. He began diligently keeping the Sabbath, Friday sunset to Saturday sunset. When there was no church to attend, he would stay at home playing an album put out by the Mormon Tabernacle Choir and read church literature all day. As a Catholic, he had collected medals and statuettes of Jesus, Mary, and various saints. These were hauled to the garbage can and destroyed. I figured this would all eventually pass. On the upside, he quit smoking; he quit going to drinking parties with his friends; and he was making some good friendships. I started getting concerned when he decided he would not graduate because the ceremony was on his Sabbath. Fortunately, his pastor told him attendance would be acceptable.

The most frightening thing was that overnight he became a Conscientious Objector. Only three months earlier he had been sitting in the Naval recruiter's office. Now he was answering questions like, "How long have you had this belief?" and "Who have you told?" Three months didn't seem like a good answer to me. A flurry of letters to his aunts and uncles written while he was filling out the application hardly seemed convincing. He was totally oblivious to what might happen if he was called before a draft board. We had heated discussions over the possible repercussions. I told him that if he was that sincere, we would move to Canada. He insisted that to run would look bad for his church and other young men seeking objector status; he would go to prison if need be. I cried, and I prayed. There must be a God. A couple months later he received his draft card, 1-O.

I was carrying a huge burden of guilt over my divorce. Betty and I were ages 14 and 17 when we married. We should never have married in the first place, but my children deserved better than what I had given them. It seems it was too late for Vicki. She was determined to go her own way. I was separated from Liz by distance. I wanted to do something for Terry. He was a good kid who, in six years, had attended eight different schools. He was a member of the National Honor Society and the high school band. His grade average placed him in the top ten percent of a graduating class of five hundred seniors.

I managed to stay in Boise for his final two years of high school, but he worked nights full-time from 4:00 p.m. to midnight during his junior year, and he pumped gas on the weekends during his senior year. Through old family connections and court appearances over compensation for my disabilities, I had shared many of my concerns with an older lawyer. He checked into Terry's school records and approached me with an unbelievable opportunity. His firm had arranged for a seven-year state appointment to Columbia College and University to be given to my son.

I cried, first for joy, and later in great disappointment. Terry refused to accept it. I knew that with his draft status he wouldn't be attending Naval Officers' Training. I didn't know he had declined his band teacher's offer to recommend him for a music scholarship at the local community college. I pleaded with him. I cried. I wanted him to be rewarded for all he had been through and accomplished. He said he wanted to be a farmer. What I didn't know was that the fundamentalist teachings he was studying had led him to believe that the whole world was under the influence of Satan: Satan's governments, Satan's churches, and Satan's universities. Universities were certain to corrupt if not destroy a young person's faith. Terry was also enthralled with prophetic speculation. He was convinced that worldwide tribulation would possibly begin as soon as 1972 and that the return of Jesus was imminent. Even if I had known, I don't think I could have swayed him.

Terry decided to attend a small Bible college in East

Texas. Over the next 25 years, that little college opened many opportunities for travel[1], marriage, and family that he may have missed had he taken a different path. Nevertheless, I still grieve when I think of what he turned down.

As soon as Terry graduated from high school, he took a summer job in Stanley, Idaho in a small sawmill. Vicki had returned to her mom. I was left with one remaining member of our family, an old Siamese cat named Sam. After two weeks by myself I decided to check on Terry. He shared a cabin that was infested with mice. His bunkmate claimed that one night the mice were scurrying on the bed when a rat jumped up and scared them off. Terry confirmed that it was nigh impossible to sleep with all the pitter-patter back and forth on the floor and scratching in the walls. I had brought Sam along, so we put him in the cabin for the night. The next morning evidence of sixteen mice in various degrees of mayhem were found strewn throughout the cabin. Sam was sprawled on the floor with a mouse-tail hanging from his mouth, so full he could barely move. The next night, the only sound in the cabin was the soft padding of paws.

That little mill was one of the most dangerous I ever saw. Men weren't wearing their hard hats or safety goggles. The ramps on either side of the massive saw blade had no safety rails to protect the operator. I talked Terry into driving to Oregon with me. He never did get paid for the two or three weeks he worked there.

I dropped Terry off at his mother's. Sam and I headed toward Salem. I was too broke to stay in a motel, but I found a campground where I could sleep in the car. A family pulled in beside me. Sam made his way to their campsite and was enjoying their kids. They played and played with that cat. I guess cats get lonely too. I left a window open for Sam that night, so he could do his business. The following morning the family was gone and so was Sam. I looked and looked, called and called. I thought, "Damn! Even the cat can't stand me." I don't think I've ever felt so bleak as when I pulled out of that campground. I hope Sam found a good home. He certainly deserved better than I could offer.

Chapter Notes

[1]Excerpts from a letter written by Gary to Terry in 1970 just before he embarked to Israel to work with a college group on an archeological dig at the Temple Mount in Jerusalem:

It takes a well-learned man to teach. I think the trip [to Israel and Europe] would do you as much good as a year of school.... You have to know people and what they are like to enable you to teach them.... Hard work and study are the making of great men. Besides, you get so much more out of life.... One thing I do know, no matter who you are or what you can do, when you're gone life still goes on. Makes one feel really small and helpless, doesn't it?

EPILOGUE FROM T.D. ROTH

When I flew to Texas in the fall of 1968, my father was only 36 years old. Dad had a passion for life and was one of those wonderful personalities that everyone seems to like. He had taken me in, then Vicki. After I left, he spent several years raising a little grandson named Christopher. I will be ever grateful that he married a young woman named Lois Rivers. She had two children, Barbara and Tim, and provided a home and family for my dad for over 43 years. Barbara once told me, "Your father was our dad." He did his best to give them what we missed.

Dad was the best salesman I've ever known and loved wheeling and dealing, buying and selling. Together with Lois, he ran a second-hand store, buying, selling, and trading everything you can imagine. If there was a good garage sale running, he was there. Often, he owned cars and trailers that he had traded for, always trading up. He told me he always carried a thousand dollars in his wallet, ready to take advantage of a good deal. He would never pay more than 50% of what something was worth and had a standard question, "How much do you need?" An example is the morning a young man wanted cash for what appeared to be a Tiffany lampshade. Dad asked, "How much do you need?" He replied, "Would $25.00 be too much?" If the lampshade had been authentic, it would have appraised between

$2,000 and $5,000. It was a gamble and certainly worth the money. Dad hung it in their sunroom content to have people think it was the real deal.

In conjunction with the store, Dad and Lois purchased a warehouse for storage of items as they came available. This allowed them to regularly restock the store. Often people lined up at the first of the month to see what new treasures had appeared. How well did they do? The store only need be open ten days per month to provide a decent lifestyle. Some think that old "horse traders" and used car salesmen are only concerned about making a dollar. Dad was different. If you had the money, he didn't mind taking it, but he also knew what it was like to be poor. If someone had a genuine need, the price dropped. A necessity, like a bed for a child, might be free.

Dad and Lois purchased and finished two large homes in Oregon, one in Dallas and the other in Gresham. They also acquired and updated DeGraff's Church Furniture in Dallas, Oregon. With Dad's experience at Marshall's, he was selling pews, chairs, and altars to churches throughout the northwest and as far away as Hawaii. When they sold the company and moved to Gresham, he set up shop to manufacture seat padding that could be installed directly into existing pews. His home-built press produced continuous padding to fit any length.

My father loved cars, especially collectibles. He was a master at repainting, reupholstering, and reselling. As many as six cars were sometimes found at his last home: three in the driveway and three more in the shop. Usually at least three of those were collectibles. The same with old boats. It seems buying and selling was in his blood. In his later years, he and Lois were members of the Edsel Owners. They traveled all over the US attending conventions. Lois is still the club treasurer, receiving calls from all over North America and parts of Western Europe. She continues to be instrumental in the club newsletters and annual convention planning.

As my father approached eighty, he made a bucket list. Lois made it happen and I went along for the ride. Every year he began planning an adventure. For me, it was a chance to make up for all I had missed as a child, also a chance to be the son I hadn't been while living in Canada. The first adventure was fishing and crabbing out of Depoe Bay on the Oregon coast. We caught our limit of ground fish and a good share of large crabs. It was a rare opportunity for fresh fried oysters. Mm, mm, mm. The next year was hot air ballooning among the fluffy clouds and blue skies of Newberg, Oregon. What a great trip! The third year, we whitewater rafted down the Deschutes River near The Dalles. We had such fun that the following day we did an advanced run on the Salmon River in Washington. The trip required wetsuits and helmets. We ran several waterfalls and shot through rapid after rapid. Poor Dad, he had forgotten the medication for his knees and was not "enjoying" himself that day. Year four, Dad flew as passenger in a two-seater glider. He wanted to take me skydiving. I told him I would go with him, but there was no way I would step out of a plane at 12,000 feet. Shortly after we talked, he dreamed that we had gone skydiving and my parachute failed to open. Skydiving was out of the question after that.

In his 80s, the deterioration of Dad's health was very noticeable from year to year. He went from occasional use of an electric scooter to continual use of a walker. His balance was getting worse and worse. Gradual heart failure was causing retention of fluids, swelling of his legs, and shortness of breath.

The summer of 2017 I spent a week with him. As soon as he heard I was coming, he began looking for some new adventure we could do. Instead, we settled for old movies, regular "old man" naps, and lots of cards. We talked about the past. He had some regrets and tears he needed to share. It was a wonderful week! We talked a little about death and I asked if he was ready. He responded, "But son, I love life!" July 13th, 2018 his heart finally gave out. I am so grateful I was there when he embraced what may be his greatest adventure of all.

Gary, Harry, and Terry (Three generations of Roths) - 1971

ABOUT THE AUTHOR

T.D. Roth grew up in southern Idaho. After high school, he graduated from Ambassador College in Southern California. Moving to Canada in the summer of 1972, Roth pastored churches in British Columbia, Saskatchewan, Ontario, and Newfoundland. He is a great story collector and currently lives in Kamloops, British Columbia. Now retired, he pursues a passion for acting, music, and writing. "The Stories of My Father" is his third published biography.

ALSO BY T.D. ROTH

THE PEASANT'S GOLD

THE STORY OF PETER WING, North America's First Chinese Mayor. Join the Wing family as they persevere through more than three decades of political and social prejudice before being recognized as "people" with the repeal of the Canadian Chinese Exclusion Act in 1947. An inspiring story of dedication and service.

DECEITFUL

WELCOME TO FLY BLOW, the haunt of a disembodied spirit seen only by Grandpa Baker who can no longer speak, and his old horse named Deceitful. Sarah Baker comes to prepare Grandpa for the old folk's home but finds herself in a web of terror and deceit.

DIABLO

THE INDIANS CALL a horse with blue eyes a Spirit or Medicine horse. His "sky-eyes" were a window to a man's soul. Let T.D. Roth carry you into the thrilling world of ranch and rodeo and Julio Ortega's ride to the death.

AS THE WINDMILL TURNS

THE MEMORIES OF WANDA BAKER is a story of love and heartache set in the turbulent years of the early twentieth century. Married at age 14 and on her own with three children at age 24, this is a poignant account of the resilience and survival of a remarkable woman.

These works are available through Amazon.com and at the Kobo Bookstore. Check out T.D.RothBooks on Facebook for more information or contact the author at tdroth216@gmail.com.

Made in the USA
Monee, IL
20 July 2020